ENGINEERING
THE PYRAMIDS

ENGINEERING
THE PYRAMIDS

DICK PARRY

SUTTON PUBLISHING

First published in 2004 by
Sutton Publishing Limited · Phoenix Mill
Thrupp · Stroud · Gloucestershire · GL5 2BU

This paperback edition first published in 2005

British Library Cataloguing in Publication Data
A catalogue record for this book is available from the British Library.

ISBN 0 7509 3415 8

Typeset in 12/16 pt Sabon.
Typesetting and origination by
Sutton Publishing Limited.
Printed and bound in England by
J.H. Haynes & Co. Ltd, Sparkford.

Contents

Preface

The three stone pyramids on the Giza plateau, visible from central Cairo, are probably the most recognisable man-made creations on earth and the most photographed. To stand beside them, even as a civil engineer, is to be awestruck at their immense size and to feel disbelief that 4,500 years ago people like ourselves could have built such structures without the technology and machines we have today. No wonder ridiculous theories such as alien builders from outer space have found gullible adherents.

For whatever reason, the ancient builders left behind no indication of the construction methods for any of the seven completed stone pyramids, in written or pictorial form, or in the physical shape of tools dating from the pyramid age. This hasn't prevented writers on the subject from disregarding the limitations posed by simple principles of engineering mechanics and making categorical statements about their construction; for instance that sleds were used to transport and raise the stone blocks, without presenting any supporting evidence and while glossing over the enormous problems attending their usage. It almost seems that something which appears in print often enough must be true, or certainly worth repeating. Of course, sleds may have been used, but they would have posed great difficulties in the creation of suitable haul roads and a practical ramp system. Any method to reduce friction, the bane of sled haulage, may have been simple in the hauling of a single sled, but could have been a nightmare with a hundred sleds or more in transit from quarry to site at any given time. Proposed ramps for raising the stones are sketched with absurd inclines of 1 in 2 or steeper, which could not have been negotiated by any method of stone haulage; and ramps are shown climbing up to 100m or more in height, having side slopes almost vertical, with no mention of what miracle material was used in their construction. The reason is simple. If sensible inclines and side slopes had been introduced into the sketches for the particular ramp configurations proposed, the ramps would have swamped the pyramids themselves. As the methods of pyramid construction were not recorded, they must have been transmitted by word of mouth and by practical demonstration, perhaps eventually coming to be known only to the priesthood, which makes the accounts of pyramid construction by Herodotus of particular interest.

The questions posed by the pyramids are endless. Were the bodies of the pharaohs really interred in them or were they an over-the-top diversionary tactic? What motivated Imhotep to extend his original mastaba for his king, to end up with the Step Pyramid? What happened at Meidum to cause its collapse and why is the Bent Pyramid bent? Why was the North Dahshur Pyramid built with much flatter slopes than the other stone pyramids? Were the shafts extending from the tomb chambers of the Great Pyramid really to facilitate the passage of Khufu's soul to its celestial abode and, if so, why did his son Khafre not build in the same provision for his own soul? Why did Menkaure build such a small pyramid in the shadow of the much larger structures of his father and grandfather? Why are no two pyramids alike, at least in detail? Fortunately, many of these questions are unlikely ever to be answered and as long as these marvellous enigmatic structures keep at least some of their secrets, our fascination for them will not cease.

Unless otherwise stated, all images have been provided by the author.

Acknowledgements

My sincere thanks go to Tom Kimura for his efforts in arranging the field tests in Japan and, of course, to the Obayashi Corporation for financing and carrying out the tests. It was a great pleasure to work with such an enlightened organisation. I am greatly indebted to Mamdouh Hamza for his unstinting help to me in making my visits to Egypt both pleasant and fruitful, and also for his suggestion that I write this book. My sincere thanks, too, to Moustafa El-Ghamrawy for the many kindnesses he has shown me on my visits to Egypt. On one of my visits to Meidum and Dahshur, I was accompanied by fellow geotechnical engineer Max Ervin, whose observations have proved very helpful, and a comfort to me. Many thanks to him and also to Christopher Feeney, Jane Entrican and Clare Jackson at Sutton Publishing for making the book a reality, and to Sarah Flight for this paperback edition.

ONE

Origins and Purpose

Throughout the more than three millennia of pharaonic rule, those Egyptians of high status who could afford it concerned themselves to an obsessive degree with their welfare in the afterlife. Leading and wealthy citizens took elaborate precautions to ensure their continued existence after death, which they believed depended upon the preservation of their earthly body. Their tombs, often constructed of stone or excavated deep into solid rock, were much more elaborate than their homes and palaces, which, for the most part, consisted of sun-dried mudbrick.

An early form of tomb was the mastaba, the name deriving from the Egyptian for a bench which it resembled in outward appearance. It consisted of a burial chamber below ground level, which housed the body, surmounted by a squat superstructure of sun-baked mudbrick containing cells intended for storage of wine jars, food-vessels, hunting implements and other necessities for enjoying the afterlife to the full. A significant development in the IV Dynasty saw stone replace brick, the interior of the superstructure often consisting of a low-grade local limestone, with an outer facing of fine quality Tura limestone.

The unification around 3100 BC of the two greatly differing geographic regions of Egypt – the elongated narrow Nile valley of the Upper, or southern, largely arid region and the fan-shaped Lower, or northern, productive marshy region – gave rise to a remarkable civilisation lasting over 3,000 years under pharaonic rule. Although the two regions continued to be administered separately, the wearing by the pharaoh of both the separate white and red crowns of Upper and Lower Egypt symbolised their unification, which remained substantially intact throughout the pharaonic period – in part attributable to the wisdom of Menes, the first pharaoh, in establishing the capital at Memphis, some 24km south of modern Cairo, and near the junction of the two regions.

Menes put in hand major construction works to fortify the city, which helped serve his own glorification and, perhaps even more important, also required a workforce of several thousand people from various parts of the country, which may well have helped cement the concept of unification. According to the Greek historian Herodotus, writing around 450 BC and quoting information given to him by priests in Egypt, Menes had Memphis built on land reclaimed from the Nile by diversion of the river from a point some 100 furlongs (20km) south of the city. A dam or embankment gave protection against flooding from the river and the city was enclosed within a white wall of limestone. These efforts were the forerunners of the great construction works to come, to include pyramids and other tombs, temples and canals.

Of the one hundred or so pyramids built in ancient Egypt only seven completed pyramids were constructed entirely of

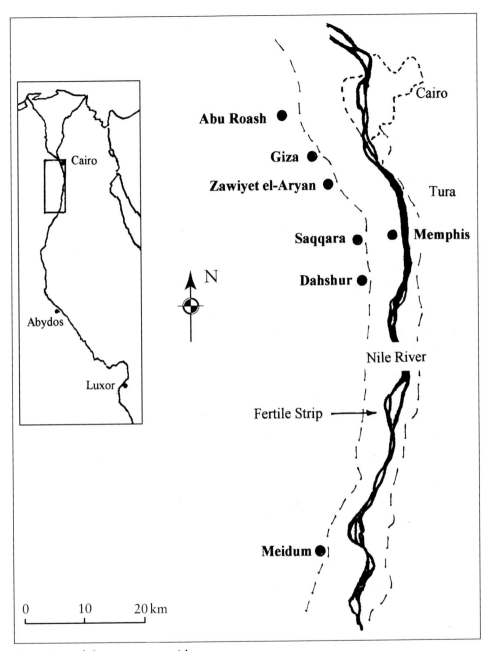

Locations of the stone pyramids.

Early Dynastic period, 2920–2575 BC		Old Kingdom, 2575–2134 BC	
I Dynasty (Menes)	2920–2770	**IV Dynasty**	2575–2465
II Dynasty	2770–2649	Snofru	2575–2551
III Dynasty	2649–2575	Khufu (Cheops)	2551–2528
Djoser	2630–2611	Ra'djedef	2528–2520
Sekhemkhet	2611–2603	Khafre (Chefren)	2520–2494
Khaba	2603–2599	Nebka?	2494–2490
Huni (?)	2599–2575	Menkaure (Mycerinus)	2490–2472
		Shepseskaf	2472–2467

well fitted stone, and all seven date from the III Dynasty (which was the last of the Early Dynastic period) and the IV Dynasty (which was the first of the Old Kingdom period). Approximate dynastic dates are given below, together with the names of the pharaohs associated with the construction of these major pyramids. Pyramids continued to be built for nearly one thousand years after the end of the IV Dynasty, but since most consisted of mudbrick with limestone casing, very few have survived in recognisable form.

Djoser had in his court the first great polymath in history, whose accomplishments in the fields of astronomy, medicine and construction led to his deification by later generations of Egyptians. His name was Imhotep. Commissioned by Djoser to build his tomb, Imhotep first constructed a mastaba of limestone blocks 63m square and 8m high, each face of which he oriented towards one of the four cardinal compass points. Viewing the completed structure, Djoser may have been less than impressed with its unspectacular appearance; as god-king of a united Egypt he must surely have felt the need for something more imposing to satisfy his ego and to protect his mortal remains. Alternatively, Imhotep himself may have had grandiose ambitions to leave behind something to be remembered by (a sentiment not unknown among architects today), and on completion of the mastaba convinced Djoser – if he needed convincing – that a much larger structure would more fittingly match the great man's stature. Imhotep extended the mastaba, first into a four-stepped pyramid and finally into a six-stepped pyramid. Technologically it was a great advance.

Once established, the pyramid form became the standard for the tombs of succeeding pharaohs. These were built largely from blocks of local limestone where available. A development after the step pyramid was an outer casing of fine Tura limestone, floated across the Nile and dressed to give a smooth exterior and thus a true pyramid. Increasingly elaborate precautions taken to thwart tomb robbers included the incorporation of multiple tomb chambers, chambers below natural ground level and within the structure, blind corridors, false entrances and stone portcullises which dropped down behind the burial parties after they had left the tomb chambers. All to no avail. Over the centuries the tomb robbers still managed to gain entry to the tomb chambers and carry off treasures of great value buried with the pharaohs – a bewildering array of priceless items intended for the pharaoh's use in the afterlife, including gold knives and gold vessels, alabaster pots, silver trinkets, gold-sheeted couches and chairs.

The pyramids were not isolated structures. They stood in the midst of attendant constructions including, in some cases, subsidiary pyramids for the queens and mastaba tombs for nobles and the pharaoh's close family members. Boat pits contained craft to convey the pharaoh to his heavenly abode and a massive limestone wall often surrounded the pyramid complex. An integral feature of each pyramid was the mortuary temple, the exact purpose of which is open to some dispute as the rooms and doorways seem to be too small for the funeral procession. Reflecting as they do some of the features of the royal palaces, they may simply have been intended to provide an eternal familiar residence for the deceased king. A sloping causeway linked the mortuary temple to the valley temple situated at the entry to the whole complex.

Whether in the mortuary temple or elsewhere, the pharaoh's body underwent lengthy ritualistic and purification processes followed by mummification before interment. These served to ensure both the afterlife of the deceased pharaoh and the transfer of his physical and spiritual powers to the new pharaoh.

The seven completed stone pyramids of the 3rd and 4th Dynasties and three uncompleted pyramids are listed below with the corresponding pharaohs and locations.

Pyramid name	Location	Pharaoh
Step Pyramid	Saqqara	Djoser
Unfinished Pyramid	Saqqara	Sekhemket
Unfinished (Layer) Pyramid	Zawiyet el-Aryan	Khaba (?)
Meidum Pyramid	Meidum	Snofru. May have been initially intended for obscure III Dynasty Pharaoh Huni
South Dahshur (Bent) Pyramid	Dahshur	Snofru
North Dahshur (Red) Pyramid	Dahshur	Snofru
Great Pyramid	Giza	Khufu
Ra'djedef Pyramid	Abu Roash	Ra'djedef
Khafre Pyramid	Giza	Khafre
Menkaure Pyramid	Giza	Menkaure

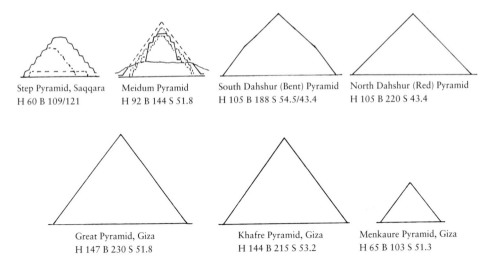

Profiles and relative sizes of the seven completed stone pyramids H= height and B= base length in metres; S= slope in degrees.

Stone pyramids of the 5th and 6th Dynasties were much inferior to their predecessors, with limestone casing covering poorly fitted smaller stones and mud mortar or debris in the gaps. Badly degraded, and some never even completed, they are not considered further here.

Apart from Djoser, the pharaoh of the Step Pyramid, the remaining four pharaohs associated with the other six completed pyramids were all in direct father–son relationships. The first of these, Snofru, was the son of Huni, the last king of the III Dynasty, a rather shadowy figure for whom the Meidum Pyramid may have been originally intended. Notwithstanding that the completion of three major stone pyramids (and one minor pyramid) during his 24-year reign must have placed an enormous strain on the resources of the country, later generations throughout pharaonic history revered the memory of Snofru, according him epithets such as 'The Beneficent King'. Clearly a very energetic ruler with a strong hold on the levers of power, he not only provided a son to be his successor, but also two of his other sons served as viziers (in effect, prime ministers) during both his reign and that of his son Khufu. He is recorded as having conducted campaigns against Libya and Nubia, in the latter case taking 7,000 prisoners to be employed on the royal estates and possibly on pyramid construction. In one single year he had forty loads of cedar wood shipped from the Lebanon port of Byblos to Egypt, most of which would have been intended for ship building and for use in pyramid construction.

In contrast to his father, Khufu suffered a tarnished reputation at the hands of later priests, who claimed that he had brought all kinds of misery down on the country, forbidden his subjects to practise their religion and closed the temples. It is possible he was confused with, or seen in the same light as, the much later New Kingdom pharaoh Akhnaten, who recognised only one god, the sun-god Aten, and consequently earned the hatred of the powerful Theban priesthood. Herodotus makes it clear he is simply recording the accounts given to him by the priests, who also told him that Khufu forced his subjects to labour as slaves on his works. There is no evidence to support any of these claims. The sheer magnitude of the Great Pyramid may have influenced the belief that he enslaved the labour force to achieve his ends, but ironically the volume of pyramid building in the reign of his much revered father exceeded that of Khufu by 40 per cent. With tongue clearly in cheek and no doubt to entertain his audience, Herodotus relates a story of how Khufu sent his daughter to a bawdy house and instructed her to charge a specific sum in order to bolster the king's dwindling finances. In addition to this charge, on her own initiative to ensure she would be remembered after her death, she asked each customer to donate a block of stone, managing to acquire sufficient of these to build the middle of the three subsidiary pyramids close to the Great Pyramid.

Khufu should have been succeeded by his eldest son Kawab, the issue of his senior queen Mertiotes, and who even married his own sister Hetpheres II to ensure his succession. But it didn't happen. By somehow disposing of Kawab, Ra'djedef, another son but by an unknown queen, succeeded his father and immediately attended to the ceremonies required to ensure Khufu's eternal life in the afterworld, and probably to buttress his own position. He reigned for only about eight years, to be usurped in turn by Khafre, another son of Khufu by yet another wife. Khafre did not see the need to complete the pyramid intended for Ra'djedef at Abu Roash, 8km to the north of the Great Pyramid, and chose to build his own pyramid immediately adjacent to that of his father, and only slightly smaller. Again, it may have been the sheer size of his pyramid which led later generations to conclude he was no less a tyrant than his father, in contrast to his own son, Menkaure, whose much smaller pyramid – and indeed the last Giza pyramid – may have served to give him a much enhanced reputation. According to the account by Herodotus, Menkaure reopened the temples, abolished slavery and had the greatest reputation for justice of all the monarchs who ruled Egypt. He obviously won the approval of the priests.

While there can be no doubt that the purpose of the pyramids was to protect forever the mortal remains of the deceased pharaoh, no identifiable body remains have been found in any of the major pyramids, added to which three pyramids are attributed to the one pharaoh, Snofru. However, two of these may have been deemed unsatisfactory to receive the remains of the god-king, the Meidum Pyramid having partially collapsed, apparently around the time of its completion, and the Bent Pyramid showing signs of settlement and structural distress during construction, to the extent that the builders hastily finished it off at a flatter slope angle to try and limit further movements. They must have been in two minds about what to do, as the structural movements continued to increase. It would have been more logical to have finished it off as a mastaba-like flat-topped structure at the height they had reached when they realised some change in design had to be instituted (presumably the height where the change in slope occurs), but the compulsion to achieve a pyramid-like shape apparently took precedence over the more logical solution. Clearly anticipating the likely reaction of the pharaoh, or perhaps by order of the pharaoh, the builders immediately put in hand the successful construction of the North Dahshur Pyramid, about 2km away from its southern neighbour, adopting the flatter slope used to finish off the Bent Pyramid. Unusually, human fragments were found in the burial chamber, but these have not been positively identified as remains from a royal mummy.

During the period of about 160 years separating the construction of the Step Pyramid from that of Menkaure's Pyramid at least two, and probably three, stone pyramids were started but never finished, and indeed very little progress was made in their construction. In each case the pharaoh for whom they were intended reigned for only a short time: eight years in the case of Sekhemkhet and Ra'djedef, four years in the case of Khaba and perhaps a similar period for the IV Dynasty Nebka, who may or may not have existed and reigned in the brief period separating Khafre and Menkaure. The seven 'completed' pyramids all belong to pharaohs who reigned for periods ranging from eighteen to twenty-six years. This suggests that the builders ceased construction if the pharaoh died before his pyramid was complete, or at least substantially complete, as the pyramid of Menkaure, who reigned for the shortest period of eighteen years, was finished off by his successor, Shepseskaf, whose own tomb took the form of a huge mastaba in South Saqqara. Although tomb chambers have been found below the unfinished pyramids, there is no evidence of any interments in these and it is highly unlikely that any use was made of them. This raises the question of what happened to the remains of the pharaohs who commissioned them; presumably these received 'lesser' burials because of, or somehow related to, the shortness of their reigns.

The possibility has been raised many times by Egyptologists and others that the pyramids had symbolisms or functions additional to, or even transcending, their obvious role as mass structures protecting the bodies of the pharaohs. Some see them as stairways by which the pharaoh's spiritual self could ascend to its heavenly abode – which raises the question of why the faces were rendered smooth, which would have made the ascent more difficult. Even more unlikely is the suggestion that they symbolise the rays of the sun breaking through cloud. In fact the pyramid form followed inevitably from considerations of structural stability, once the decision had been made to upgrade from the bench-like mastabas to huge towering structures of masonry to protect the bodies of the pharaohs.

Adopting the pyramid form rather than building higher and higher mastabas, with their vertical or near-vertical sides, offered several advantages, doubtless well known to the ancient builders. Despite a partial collapse at Meidum the pyramid shape is fundamentally the most stable practical form which can be achieved with mass masonry construction. Furthermore, for specific base and height dimensions, it uses a minimum of masonry, and the quantity required diminishes rapidly with height, so that only a small amount has to be lifted to the upper parts of the structure. When the pyramid has reached one-third of its height, two-thirds of the masonry has already been placed; and when it reaches mid-height, 87 per cent has been placed. The complete lack of records relating to their construction suggests that the Egyptians simply viewed the pyramids as mass masonry structures to protect the mortal remains of the pharaoh, but with no religious significance in themselves.

Although the masonry masses of the pyramids may not have had any religious purpose their contents certainly did, a factor which may conceivably have had an important bearing on the selection of sites for their construction. A plausible argument has been put forward by Bauval and Gilbert that the dispositions of the three major pyramids on the Giza plateau correspond to the relative positions of the three stars in Orion's belt and, further, that the brightness of the individual stars corresponds to the sizes of the pyramids. The importance of this observation lies in the fact that the Orion constellation is associated with the Egyptian god Osiris. Bauval and Gilbert also point out that so-called ventilation shafts in the Great

Pyramid, emanating from the tomb chambers, are aligned to the constellations of Orion and Sirius, the latter being associated with the goddess Isis, the wife of Osiris. These shafts would have facilitated the ascent of the souls of the dead to their permanent celestial abodes.

While there may be some strength in these arguments, they are based on selected evidence. There are stars in the Orion constellation with no corresponding pyramids and pyramids with no corresponding stars. Also, why are there no 'ventilation shafts' in other pyramids? Did the souls of their occupants not deserve to have their passage to their celestial abodes facilitated in this way?

TWO

Evolution in Pyramid Design

When Djoser's engineer Imhotep undertook the task of converting the pharaoh's intended mastaba into a much larger structure, he had no existing example of a mass masonry structure on which to base his design. This was the first massive masonry structure ever to be built. Although in common with all the pyramids, and indeed practically all other ancient Egyptian tombs, the Step Pyramid failed in its purpose of protecting forever both the pharaoh's remains and the objects accompanying him in his afterlife, Imhotep succeeded magnificently in creating a structure both massive and stable, and one which remains substantially intact to this day. A modern civil engineer, armed with mathematics, mechanics and the laws of physics, plus millennia of building technology as guidance, might well adopt the same solution.

Initially, Imhotep built a four-step structure, but perhaps spurred by its successful completion, he extended it to six steps. This consisted of a 60m high central core of rough stone blocks with planar sides having an angle to the horizontal of about 75°, the core supported by a series of accretion or buttress walls lying against it, also with slope angles of 75°, and terminating at successively lower heights as distance from the core increased. This resulted in a stable structure of a stepped pyramid form, with the tops of the buttress walls, which outwardly slope downwards (presumably to shed water), forming the steps. With this example before them, builders of pyramids immediately succeeding this chose to adopt the same design, but the first two of these, that for Sekhemkhet close to the Step Pyramid and the Layer Pyramid about 7km to the north, were abandoned early in their construction, possibly because of the premature deaths of their intended occupants.

The second pyramid to be completed, or substantially completed, poses two questions. Why was it sited at Meidum, a remote area over 50km south of the capital Memphis, and why was it one of three constructed, or at least completed, for the IV Dynasty pharaoh, Snofru? The answer to the first question is likely to remain a mystery, but the second can be plausibly attributed to its collapse, which Snofru may have taken to be a bad omen, an indication from the gods of their disapproval at his having appropriated the pyramid for himself rather than completing it for his predecessor, Huni, for whom some Egyptologists believe it was originally intended. The damage to the pyramid that immediately followed its partial collapse was probably much less than is visible today, after four and a half millennia of assault by the elements on the weakened structure; and, even more important, after the destruction wrought by the quarrying activities to which Petrie, the 'Father of Egyptology', drew attention in his descriptions of the results of his excavations at the site. It is

Imhotep extended the originally intended mastaba for the tomb of Pharaoh Djoser into first a four-step, then a six-step pyramid to create the world's first major stone structure.

The buttress wall design pioneered by Imhotep in the Step Pyramid – with the height of the inclined walls decreasing with distance away from the core – led inevitably to the pyramid shape. Unfortunately, the interfaces between the walls, such as that shown here, introduced inherent weaknesses into the structure.

likely that the damage could have been repaired at the time of its occurrence to give a stable, if slightly modified, structure, but Snofru eschewed this course of action in favour of moving 45km north to construct the second pyramid attributed to him, at South Dahshur. In fact, if Mendelssohn, who spent ten years studying the Meidum Pyramid, is correct, the builders had already made considerable headway with the construction of this more northerly pyramid when the Meidum collapse occurred, the overlap in construction ensuring continuity in the utilisation of the workforce.

The buttress wall design of the Meidum Pyramid followed closely that of its Saqqaran predecessor, its initial seven steps subsequently being increased to eight. A decision made on, or very near to, its completion to add an outer coating layer of stones to give planar sloping faces, and thus produce a true pyramid, went disastrously wrong. It led ultimately to its present-day appearance, clearly visible from the Desert Highway: a massive stepped tower of stone protruding above an apparent mound of sand and rubble, which, in fact, consists mainly of the lower intact portion of the pyramid obscured by the sand and rubble which lie against it. The changes in design late in the seven- and eight-step construction phases introduced serious weaknesses into the structure, which led to the partial collapse. Towards or at the end of these construction phases the outer exposed step faces were smoothed off, either for appearance purposes or to shed water. These became incorporated within the structure as further construction proceeded, giving low-friction interfaces within it that introduced serious weaknesses. The collapse, when it came, may have been caused quite simply by the incumbent weight of the added outer surface layers, or it may

Meidum Pyramid
collapsed because
the inherent
weaknesses in the
buttress wall
design made it
unable to sustain
the weight of the
outer surface
layer, which was
added to give
smooth outer
faces to the
structure.

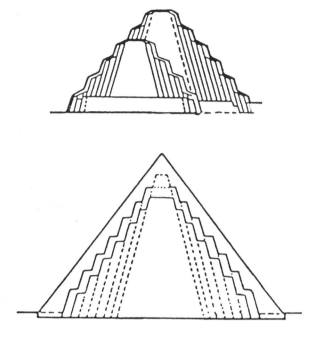

Buttress wall design for step pyramid and Meidum Pyramid.

have been triggered by a natural event such as an earth tremor or heavy rain. Bands of smoothed stones, originally intended as outer exposed faces, are still clearly visible on the surface of the stone tower.

The builders of the South Dahshur Pyramid adopted the same basic design with buttress walls as for the Meidum Pyramid, but again changes appear to have been made during construction, the initial structure having a base area smaller than that seen today, with slopes of perhaps 60°. Built over a clay layer rather than solid rock, the pyramid exhibits clear evidence of uneven settlements leading to structural distress, manifest in the cracking and block displacements seen in the tomb chambers and their access passages and manifest, too, in

Unable to stop severe movements occurring within the structure of the South Dahshur (Bent) Pyramid, arising from weak foundation strata, the builders hastily finished it off at a flatter angle.

the great cedar beams which the ancient builders inserted to shore up and reinforce the upper burial chamber.

Alarmed by the increasingly obvious signs of movements as construction progressed, and perhaps mindful of the Meidum collapse, the builders extended the base dimensions in order to surround the initial structure with a girdle of stone sloping at a reduced angle of slightly less than 55°. At the lower levels these stones were set with an inward slope, presumably in the belief that this would give added stability, suggesting that the

Inward sloping outer
casing blocks and
smoothed facing of South
Dahshur (Bent) Pyramid.
Much of the smoother
outer facing of this
pyramid remains intact.

builders were unaware that they had foundation rather than structural problems; when the movements continued they reverted to laying these outer stones horizontally in the higher layers. Eventually, when their various measures to arrest the movements failed, they finished the pyramid off at the lesser slope of 43.5° to reduce further weight additions on the defective structure. It would have been more logical to have finished it as a flat-topped structure, but perhaps the need to achieve a pyramid shape, however flawed, was too entrenched even to contemplate this.

The depth of concern on the part of Pharaoh Snofru and his advisors when the builders, probably with reluctance and after some delay, confessed to the continuing problems they were having at South Dahshur, can only be imagined, the Meidum Pyramid having already been abandoned after its catastrophic failure. A solution had to be found, and quickly. Great civil engineering structures and works around the world today, including bridges, dams and buildings, owe their success in no small part to lessons learned from past failures. It is greatly to the credit of these ancient builders that they learned the lessons of their mistakes, and those of their predecessors at Meidum and South Dahshur, enabling them to produce a stable design of true pyramid form.

Abandoning the concept of a central core and buttress walls, the builders now adopted a coursed form of construction, building the pyramid up tier by tier, each tier consisting of a single layer of blocks uniform in thickness across the full width of the structure, but with some variation in thickness from layer to layer. Greater care in dressing and placing the blocks reduced the need to fill gaps between blocks, particularly in the interior masonry, with rubble or clay mortar, and with only the occasional gypsum mortar. Apparently exercising understandable caution, the builders adopted the conservative slope angle of 43.5° used to finish off the Bent Pyramid, although the flatter slope angle may also have been adopted to ensure rapid completion of a structure fit to receive the body of the god-king, rather than solely for considerations of stability.

With the successful completion of the North Dahshur Pyramid the builders of the Great Pyramid on the Giza plateau for Snofru's son, Khufu, returned to their preferred slope angle of 52°. This represents a height to base ratio equivalent to four diameters of a cylinder to its circumference, a characteristic that has prompted some modern writers to speculate that rolling cylinders may have been used in determining pyramid geometry. The fact that the flatter angle of the North Dahshur Pyramid, and that used to finish off the Bent Pyramid, has the ratio of three diameters to the circumference is seen to lend some support to this argument. The Great Pyramid has only a slightly longer base length of 230m compared to 220m for the North Dahshur Pyramid, but its volume of nearly 2.6 million cubic metres is 50 per cent greater. A small part of this is made up by a knoll of rock on which the pyramid is built and it is usually assumed that the structure consists of about 2.3 million limestone blocks with an average volume of 1 cubic metre each and weighing some 2.5 tonnes. With the exception of larger blocks in the base layer, the biggest limestone blocks employed were casing blocks two to three times the average size, which were trimmed as the final operation in the building of the pyramid to give it a smooth exterior. These have long since been quarried by later generations of builders. Much larger were the granite blocks from Aswan used in the construction of the King's Chamber, the largest having a thickness of 1.3m, width 1.8m and length 8m, weighing

Following the catastrophic collapse at Meidum and the structural distortions at South Dahshur, the builders of the North Dahshur (Red) Pyramid abandoned buttress walls in favour of layered construction. They also cautiously adopted the flatter face angle used to finish off its South Dahshur neighbour.

With confidence restored after the successful completion of the North Dahshur Pyramid, Khufu's builders opted for layered construction and returned to the favoured steeper slope angle of about 52°. Although its base lengths of 230m are only slightly greater than the 220m of the North Dahshur Pyramid, the Great Pyramid exceeds by 50 per cent the volume of its immediate predecessor.

over 50 tonnes. While local quarries supplied much of the limestone used in the interior of the pyramid, the better quality limestone needed for the outer casing blocks had to be brought from the Tura quarries on the other side of the Nile.

Measurements made by Petrie showed the Great Pyramid to consist of 203 courses, fluctuating in thickness through the height of the structure in response to conditions in the quarries, but generally decreasing from nearly 1.5m at the base to 0.5m approaching the top. As the slopes are 52°, the superficial form of the pyramid faces before trimming would have been a series of steps having widths ranging from 1.4m to 0.4m and averaging 0.6m. These widths are significant, as use may have been made of the steps in raising the stones into position.

In his account of the building of the Great Pyramid, Herodotus gives the construction time as twenty years, and this period, or a few years longer at most, is accepted by most Egyptologists today. This means that the 2.3 million blocks were placed at an average rate of one every two

Stone tiers or layers in the Great Pyramid.

minutes throughout the construction period, utilising all the hours of daylight; and peak rates during construction of the lower portions of the pyramid must have been more like one block placed every minute. Furthermore, the three pyramids preceding it, all attributed to Snofru, would have required the same or even quicker rate of placement, and the rate would have been maintained with the construction of Khafre's pyramid adjacent to the Great Pyramid on the Giza plateau.

Khufu's successor, his son Ra'djedef, ruled for only eight years, which may be why little progress was made in the construction of his pyramid at Abu Roash, 8km to the north

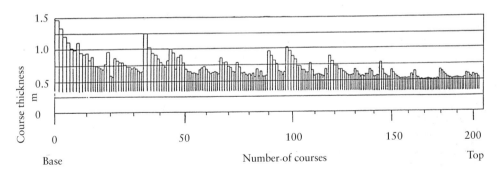

The fluctuating thicknesses of layers in the Great Pyramid, as measured by Petrie, probably reflect strata thicknesses encountered in the quarrying operations.

of Giza, before it was abandoned. The small amount of core masonry and larger amounts of granite casing blocks seen at the site today give little indication of the architectural form intended for the structure.

Whatever reason Ra'djedef had for picking the site at Abu Roash his successor Khafre, also a son of Khufu, did not share it, choosing instead to site his pyramid at Giza, in close proximity to his father's pyramid. Its side slopes of just over 53° are marginally steeper and the base lengths of 215m are some 15m shorter than the corresponding ones for his father's monument, but Khafre compensated for its slightly smaller mass by establishing it on a site 10m higher than the founding level of the Great Pyramid. A visible feature of Khafre's pyramid is the survival of some of the smoothed casing stones at its tip. Its construction seems to have largely copied that of its immediate completed predecessor, except for the use of granite casing blocks in the lowest layer; these may originally have been destined for Ra'djedef's aborted structure.

33

Built in close proximity to his father's pyramid, Khafre compensated for its slightly smaller size by founding his pyramid on a site 10m higher than the Great Pyramid.

Smoothed casing stones at the tip of Khafre's pyramid.

Although Khafre's son Menkaure did not immediately succeed his father, he did become pharaoh after a period of four years under the rule of his cousin, the son of Ra'djedef. He followed his father in having his pyramid built on the Giza site, but, with base dimensions only a little over 100m in length and slightly reduced side slopes, it has a volume only about one-tenth of its massive neighbours, and he may have initially intended something even smaller. Space restrictions on the Giza plateau may have forced Menkaure to think small, but the enormous strain and drain on the country's manpower and economic resources over 150 years of pyramid building must surely have been a determining factor as well, or perhaps

36

The whole of Egypt probably breathed a sigh of relief when Menkaure opted for (or was persuaded to agree to) a pyramid only about one-tenth the volume of its two immediate predecessors. However, he surfaced the lower portion with granite blocks from Aswan, which were much more difficult to quarry, work and transport than limestone blocks.

the god-king's advisors realised the country was simply growing weary of constructing these ego-flattering behemoths. Menkaure didn't entirely stint himself, however, surfacing the lower portion of the pyramid with granite blocks from Aswan, or perhaps he simply removed them from Ra'djedef's unfinished pyramid at Abu Roash. The three subsidiary queens' pyramids alongside this one match the number at the Great Pyramid. Menkaure's pyramid, completed after his death by his successor Shepseskaf, marked the end of stone pyramid building, Shepseskaf himself choosing to be buried at South Saqqara in a huge mudbrick mastaba encased in fine limestone, with a bottom course of red granite.

Pyramids continued to be built in Egypt for another eight hundred years or so right up to the end of the Middle Kingdom period, but their inferior construction deteriorated rapidly, particularly when protective outer limestone casing was removed for various building purposes, and most are not even recognisable to the untutored eye today.

THREE

The Tomb Chambers

The Step Pyramid is underlain by a labyrinth of tunnelled galleries and chambers, nearly 6km in total length, connecting to a central vertical shaft 7m square and 28m deep, providing room not only for the body of the pharaoh, but also for his family members and, in keeping with mastaba customs, space for storage of food and offerings. A sloping passage links the central shaft to a trench dug into the natural ground at the northern edge of the pyramid. It superseded an earlier stairway with an entrance in the northern face of the pyramid, which became inaccessible with the extension of the pyramid from four to six steps. Pink granite blocks from Aswan, and a 3.5 tonne granite plug, enclosed and sealed the king's tomb chamber located at the base of the shaft. Tomb chamber entrances sited on the northern faces became standard for all the subsequent stone pyramids.

In contrast to its Saqqara predecessor, the solution adopted at Meidum could hardly have been simpler: the access passage, with its entrance one-fifth its height up the north face, angles down through the pyramid structure into the underlying rock, where it levels out and continues to the bottom of a short vertical shaft leading upwards to the tomb chamber, founded at the base of the pyramid structure. Side recesses in the level portion of the shaft may have been used to store stone blocks to seal the chamber, while timber baulks found embedded in the walls of the shaft were probably intended for use in raising the sarcophagus into the chamber. The absence of a sarcophagus in the chamber confirms the likelihood that the pyramid collapsed on or near completion, leading to its abandonment. The use of corbelling to roof the tomb chamber introduced an elegant architectural and engineering feature into pyramid design, the technique consisting of each layer of stone projecting beyond the layer below it until the roof was closed, or sufficiently narrow to be easily spanned by stone slabs. This directed the weight of the overlying structure away from the tomb chamber, and avoided the need to use massive beams to span the opening.

The Bent Pyramid is unique in having a tomb passage with an entry from the west face as well as from the north face; again, this innovation may have been a reaction by the builders to the movements occurring in the structure. The original passage angles down from its entrance in the north face, located 12m above the base, through the pyramid structure into the underlying deformable clay deposits to the

Opposite: The Step Pyramid is underlain by a labyrinth of tunnelled galleries and chambers, nearly 6km in total length, connecting to a central vertical shaft 7m square and 28m deep, providing room not only for the body of the pharaoh, but also for his family members and, in keeping with mastaba customs, space for storage of food and offerings. (*Reproduced from* The Pyramids of Egypt, *by I.E.S. Edwards, Penguin Books, courtesy Penguin Group UK*)

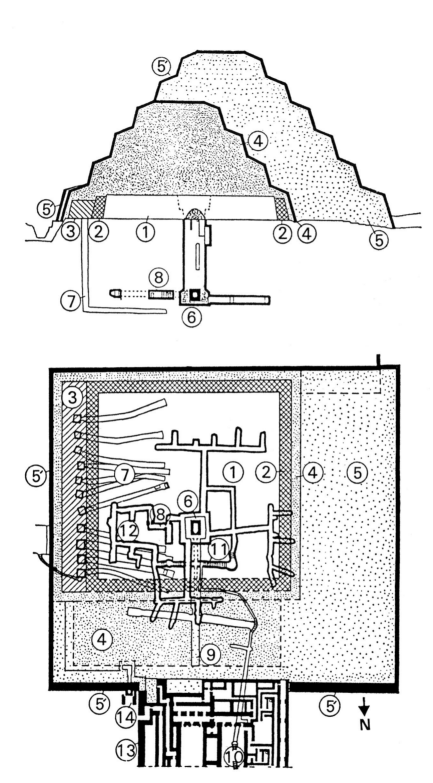

A short length of the 6km of tunnelled galleries below the Step Pyramid. (*Ancient Egypt Picture Library*)

base of a narrow corbelled antechamber, from the top of which access is gained to the original tomb chamber, 5m wide and 6.25m long. The roof of this impressive chamber was formed by corbelling the top fifteen courses of both the end walls and side walls, giving a total height from floor level of 17.4m. The top coincides with the original ground level. Squared holes in the walls of the antechamber were probably intended to take cedar beams to be used in raising the sarcophagus into the tomb chamber.

Cracking and block displacements, which can be seen in the access passage as well as the antechamber and its connecting tomb chamber, are symptomatic of the movements which

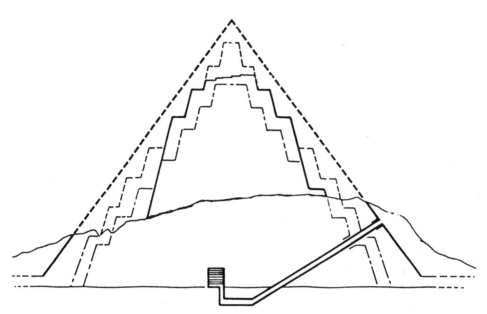

Although the single-chamber solution at Meidum contrasted with tomb arrangements for most of the other stone pyramids, it set the precedent for others by having the entrance to its access shaft in the north face and angling down at a slope of 1 in 2. The corbelled roof design was copied in more sophisticated forms in the Dahshur tomb chambers and in the Grand Gallery of the Great Pyramid.

would have caused increasing consternation and puzzlement on the part of the builders, because settlements in clay can continue over long periods even under a constant load. So even if they halted construction for a time, as they may well have done, the settlements would have continued to increase. At some stage a decision must have been made to abandon this tomb chamber in favour of a location within the structure of the pyramid, in the apparent belief (or hope?) that the deformation would be confined to the lower part of the pyramid and in the underlying clay. If so, this was a

The Egyptians first used corbelled roof construction in the burial chamber of the Meidum Pyramid. The technique consists of progressively reducing the gap between opposite walls by projecting each stone layer beyond the inner edge of the layer below it. The roof may be formed above a rectangular chamber by corbelling one pair of opposite walls, as here, or by corbelling both pairs of opposite walls. (*Ancient Egypt Picture Library*)

The Tomb Chambers

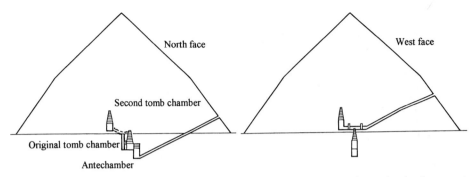

The South Dahshur Pyramid has, uniquely, tomb entrances from both the north and west faces. The original entrance from the north face connects to a corbelled antechamber, from near the top of which entry is gained to the original corbelled tomb chamber. The second, almost identical, tomb chamber, together with its entry from the west face, may have been built in response to the observed movements in the structure.

misunderstanding of the way a structure deforms when its foundations settle. The higher chamber, also with a lofty corbelled roof, is accessed from the west face of the pyramid by a sloping passage, in which recesses were cut to contain portcullis blocking stones which could be slid into position. A rough passage of uncertain date links the two tomb chambers. The builders plastered the cracks in both chambers to no avail and, in a desperate bid to stabilise the upper chamber, shored it up with a framework of cedar timbers.

In a departure from previous practice, the builders of the North Dahshur Pyramid founded the tomb chamber and access system entirely within the pyramid structure, a decision which may have been forced on them by the need to complete quickly a structure suitable to house the body of the ageing pharaoh, giving them no time to make excavations into the natural rock before starting construction.

Corbelled roof in tomb
antechamber of South Dahshur
Pyramid.

Alternatively, or even as an additional reason to adopt this
solution, they may, with some justification, have blamed the
problems experienced with the South Dahshur Pyramid on
the weakening of the underlying natural material by the deep
excavations made into it. From its entrance in the north face,
the access passage slopes downwards at the usual angle
adopted by the builders of about 1:2 (i.e. one vertical to two
horizontal) until it reaches the base of the pyramid, where it
levels out before entering the first of two almost identical
interconnected corbelled antechambers, 9.5m long by 3.6m
wide, the second lying directly below the apex of the
pyramid. The corbelled tomb chamber itself, slightly larger
than the lower antechambers with its imposing height of

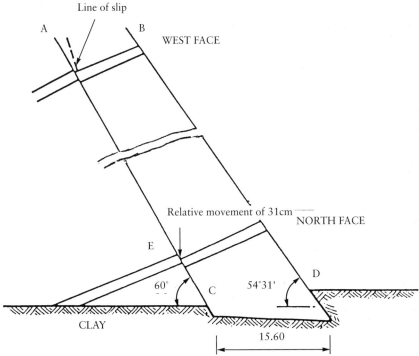

Structural displacements in tomb access passages of South Dahshur Pyramid caused by foundation settlements. (*Kerisel*)

14.7m, is reached by a short passage opening into the south wall of the second antechamber, 7.5m above floor level. Some fragments of human remains, of uncertain origin, were found in the chamber.

The seemingly haphazard arrangement of corridors, shafts and openings in the Great Pyramid suggests that the builders changed their minds at least twice before fixing on the final location of the King's Chamber high up in the pyramid structure; but this view is challenged by Mark Lehner on the basis that the provision of three chambers had almost become

47

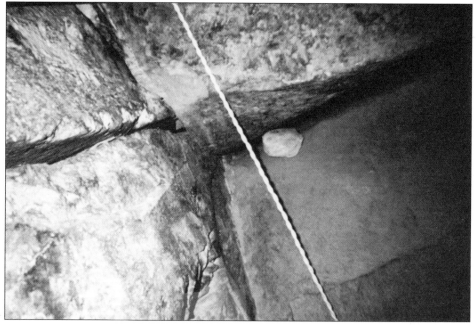

Displacement of blocks in lower access passage of South Dahshur Pyramid.

the rule for Old Kingdom pyramids. The unfinished nature of the lowest chamber in the virgin rock, likened by Edwards to a quarry, hardly supports this. From the entrance in the north face nearly 17m above ground level, a corridor descends at a slope of about 1:2 through the pyramid structure deep into the underlying rock, before levelling out at a depth of about 30m below the plateau surface to access an unfinished chamber. An ascending corridor nearly 40m in length, with the familiar 1:2 slope, leaves the descending corridor about 18m from the pyramid entrance, and terminates at a three-way junction, whence a level corridor leads to the second chamber, wrongly called the Queen's Chamber. The junction is also the entry point to the Grand Gallery, an awe-inspiring corbelled passage

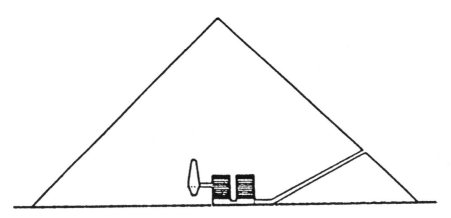

Access to the corbelled tomb chamber of the North Dahshur Pyramid is through two antechambers, also corbelled, all founded within the structure of the pyramid.

of smoothed limestone, 8.5m high, with its top 1m in width spanned by overlapping roofing slabs. The slope of the Grand Gallery, 46.5m in length, continues that of the ascending corridor until it reaches a high step giving access to a restricted passage leading into the King's Chamber.

The King's Chamber itself is a complete departure from its predecessors, first in being built entirely of granite and second in having a roof not of corbelled construction, but of nine granite beams making up the 10.5m by 5.2m roof area, each spanning the full width, and in total weighing some 400 tonnes. Above this, five hollow compartments relieve weight on the tomb chamber itself, each separated by horizontal layers of granite beams, which also form the peaked roof of the top chamber. Egyptologists accessing these compartments in the nineteenth century, by hollowing a shaft from below, found some of the walls to be of undressed limestone with quarry markings still on them, including the only example of

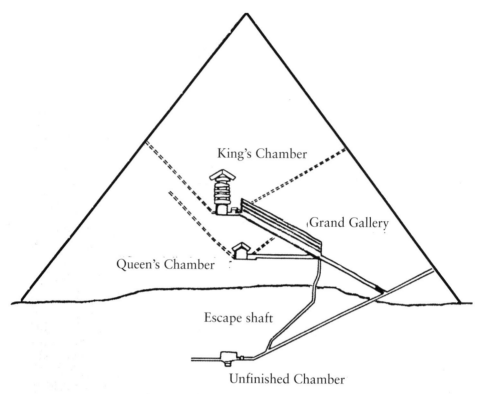

King's Chamber

Grand Gallery

Queen's Chamber

Escape shaft

Unfinished Chamber

Having abandoned an unfinished tomb chamber excavated into the natural rock, the builders of the Great Pyramid built two chambers within the structure itself, the lower one wrongly called the Queen's Chamber and the upper one the King's Chamber. The King's Chamber is unique in being built entirely of granite, topped by a vertical succession of load-relieving chambers formed by massive granite beams spanning the 5.2m width of the chamber, the topmost one having a peaked granite roof. Shafts angling up from the two chambers are thought by some to have significant stellar alignments.

the pharaoh's name found in the pyramid. The width of the granite sarcophagus, still present in the King's Chamber, slightly exceeds that of the tomb entrance, so that it must have been placed during pyramid construction. Granite plugs were used to block the immediate entrance to the tomb as well as

Although built 4,500 years ago, the Grand Gallery of the Great Pyramid remains one of the world's great architectural achievements.

Stone slabs span the corbelled walls to form the roof of the Grand Gallery.

the entrance to the ascending corridor, the dimensions of the latter such that they must have been stored in the Grand Gallery and slid down the corridor once the body had been placed in the tomb. The workers then escaped down a shaft running from the junction of the Grand Gallery and ascending corridor to the descending corridor a few metres before it enters the subterranean chamber.

In the north and south walls of the King's Chamber, small rectangular apertures, 220mm by 230mm, give access to shafts which run up at angles of 31° and 45° respectively right through the mass of masonry to the pyramid faces. Based on the observed alignments of these shafts, respectively, to the circumpolar stars and Orion's belt, which the Egyptians associated with the god Osiris, it has been proposed by Bauval and others that these were intended to facilitate the passage of the pharaoh's astral spirit to its heavenly abode. Bauval and Gilbert have pointed out that similar shafts emanating from the Queen's Chamber align with the circumpolar stars and with Sirius, the latter considered of particular significance as the Egyptians associated Sirius with the goddess Isis, the wife of Osiris. However, these shafts do not extend to the pyramid surface, and Egyptologists do not believe this to be the burial chamber of a queen. In 1993 Rudolf Gantenbrink, a German robotics engineer, sent a tiny robot fitted with a video camera up the southern shaft of the Queen's chamber, where it came to a halt after 65m in front of a blocking plug with two copper pins projecting from it and a tantalising gap underneath it. A second robot sent up in September 2002 drilled a hole through the plug, allowing access for a camera, which revealed nothing more than a small recess behind the plug, backed by a sheer stone wall. The pyramids do not yield their secrets easily.

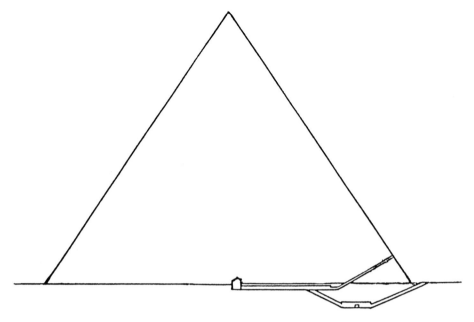

Khafre's modest single-tomb chamber has two entrances, one accessed from the north face of the pyramid and the other from ground level.

The question inevitably arises why Khufu was the only king for whom such shafts were constructed to facilitate the passage of his spirit to the stars.

Whatever the reason for the construction of three chambers in the Great Pyramid, Khufu's son Khafre did not feel the need to follow this example and restricted himself to a single tomb chamber, 14.1m long and 5m wide. This chamber was sunk into the bedrock at the centre of the pyramid base, the peaked roof similar in construction to that of his father's King's Chamber, but of limestone beams, projecting into the base of the pyramid's structure, giving the chamber a height of 6.8m. Curiously, the chamber has two entrances. One is in the north

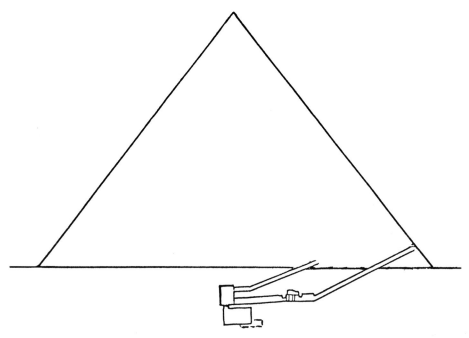

Menkaure's tomb is conventionally accessed from the north face of the pyramid and features a horizontal section with three portcullises, leading to the antechamber. The roof of the tomb chamber has the form of a granite barrel vault.

face of the pyramid, about 11.5m above base level, accessing a corridor initially descending at a slope of about 1:2, then joining with a long horizontal corridor sunk into the surface of the bedrock and leading to the tomb chamber. The second entrance is at ground level and accesses a corridor which dips initially to a short horizontal section, then rises until it joins the longer horizontal corridor. A small subsidiary chamber, possibly used for storage purposes, adjoins the short horizontal section. The tomb chamber contains a black granite sarcophagus.

There seems to have been a compulsion on the part of each pharaoh or his advisors to arrange the system of tomb chamber or chambers, corridors and accesses to be different to any in the previous pyramids, perhaps to try and foil tomb robbers, and this continued to the last of the stone pyramids, that of Menkaure. The conventional north face entrance and 1:2 descending corridor give access to a small panelled chamber hollowed out from the underlying rock, whence a horizontal corridor featuring three portcullises leads to an antechamber, 14.2m by 3.8m in plan and 4.9m high, with its long axis aligned east–west. A second 1:2 sloping corridor with a short horizontal section enters the antechamber at a higher level, but was abandoned before it penetrated the pyramid structure.

A short passage descending from the floor of the ante-chamber accesses the granite-lined tomb chamber, which has dimensions 6.6m by 2.6m in plan and 3.4m high. Another smaller chamber is situated to the right of the short passage and has access to it where it becomes horizontal, immediately before entering the tomb chamber. The ceiling of the tomb chamber has the form of a barrel vault, which is actually carved into tilted granite slabs giving a peaked roof. A handsome sarcophagus externally decorated with niches and panelling, removed from the tomb chamber in the nineteenth century, now lies at the bottom of the Mediterranean where it sank en route to England.

FOUR

Basic Aids to Construction

Creation of the stone pyramids was a remarkable achievement in design, in their precise measurements and alignments and in their construction, and yet there are no known records of the technology available to the builders, despite the fact that the Egyptians had a written language and often depicted their activities, although perhaps mostly those of the great and the good and those with influence, on the walls of temples and tombs. Any attempts to explain how the ancient engineers built these pyramids are inevitably speculative, but this can be leavened a bit by having regard to the art of the possible and an appreciation of some simple engineering mechanics. Most of what is known today about Egyptian technology comes from New Kingdom finds or later, but that does not exclude the possibility that they were in use during the Old Kingdom period, a thousand years and more earlier. After all, handcarts and the wheelbarrow, both of whose origins are very ancient, are still in use today.

Unlike their counterparts in Western Europe, who were erecting large megalithic structures at the same time, the

Egyptian builders during the Old Kingdom had at least one metal at their disposal for their construction tools, namely copper. They probably knew of iron through the finding of meteorites, but although iron ore was more plentiful than copper ore and not much more difficult to smelt, they did not appreciate that, to be malleable, iron had to be hammered while hot, whereas copper could be cold-hammered. A certain caution should be exercised in asserting this lack of knowledge because the British Museum has in its possession a small iron plate which Howard Vyse claimed to have found during the course of his 1836–7 excavations at the Great Pyramid, wedged within the masonry where the shaft from the King's Chamber exits the southern face of the pyramid. There is a strong view, however, that this find may be fraudulent. Petrie, in his writings, is non-committal about the likelihood that this is a bona fide discovery, but avers that a lump of iron wrapped up with copper axes of the VI Dynasty found in the foundations of the Abydos temples is genuine, 'absolutely certain and not open to any doubt'.

Whatever their knowledge of iron, the engineers of the time seem to have made little or no use of it, whereas they used copper to make a variety of tools, including axes, adzes, chisels, picks and saws. As limestone, a relatively soft rock, makes up most of the mass of masonry in the pyramids, copper tools would have coped quite well; but there are substantial amounts of the much harder granite in some of the structures and copper tools working it would have deteriorated very rapidly. It is difficult to take seriously suggestions that the ancient Egyptians had a technique for tempering copper to harden it, which has since been lost. For sawing and grinding the rock, an abrasive powder such as

The ancient Egyptians made good-quality rope from date palm and other plant fibres and even animal hair. This example is in the Cairo Museum.

emery or finely ground quartz sand could have been used, embedded in the teeth of a copper saw as proposed by Petrie or simply mixed with water and fed into the saw cut.

While there is much debate and disagreement on the way ancient peoples could have transported and raised, or erected, large stone blocks or megaliths, there is agreement that these tasks could not have been undertaken without one essential man-made commodity, namely some form of rope. Rope-making by twisting plant fibres or animal hair is one of man's oldest technological achievements, probably dating back to Palaeolithic times. The Egyptians made rope mainly from date palm, but other fibre sources included flax, grass, halfa, papyrus and camel hair. Ropes of papyrus fibre, 65mm in diameter, found in the Tura limestone underground quarries consist of three strands, each strand having some forty yarns, and each yarn about seven fibres. Tensile tests by Cotterell and Kamminga on palm fibre ropes, still made and used in Egyptian villages, gave strengths of about 16 MPa, so that the Tura papyrus ropes, if comparable in strength with the palm fibre ropes, would have been able to sustain a force of about 5 tonnes. There is also evidence that the Egyptians made rope by twisting or plaiting leather strips.

As the most basic device offering mechanical advantage to augment human power, the lever undoubtedly found widespread use in ancient societies committed to monumental construction works. The mechanical advantage of a lever, used as a lifting device, is given by the ratio of the relative distances from the fulcrum of the applied force and the object to be lifted. Provided there is something against which to react, levers can also be used to move blocks sideways, or slew them around, or tilt them, for example, to prise them free in the quarry from the underlying parent rock.

The wheel is regarded as one of the most fundamental and important inventions made by mankind, but there is very little evidence of its use by Egyptians in the Old Kingdom period. Proof that they knew of the wheel is demonstrated by a representation dating from the Old Kingdom, in the tomb of Kaemhesit at Saqqara, showing men climbing a scaling ladder fitted with solid wheels at its base. The wheels made the ladder highly manoeuvrable, but rather unstable when in use, which accounts for the need to have men at the bottom with long poles, as shown in the illustration, to keep it from moving. The Egyptians of this period also used the potter's wheel.

The wheel was known to Egyptians of the Old Kingdom, as shown by this V Dynasty scaling ladder, but was of little use in the loose desert sands and soft alluvial plains.

Donkeys could go where the wheel could not and were the primary means of local portage in the Old Kingdom, as they are today.

The wheel would have had very limited application in a country which, for long-distance transportation, made full use of its most valuable asset, the Nile. For local transportation and carriage of goods, such as taking farm produce to market, human portage and pack animals, particularly donkeys, were used, as they are today. Wheeled vehicles would not have been suitable for traversing either the soft silty agricultural land or the desert sands, whereas humans and pack animals could pick their way along well-worn and compacted tracks. In the building of the pyramids, hardened tracks or roads would have been required to link the quarries to the construction sites, but it would have been impossible to have constructed wooden-wheeled carts capable of carrying the huge stones.

FIVE

Construction Preliminaries and Operations

In view of the immense amount of work involved in the construction of an Old Kingdom stone pyramid, planning must have commenced immediately upon the pharaoh's accession. Imhotep and his successors would have presented the newly installed pharaoh and his closest advisors with a design intended to ensure the everlasting protection and preservation of the god-king's earthly remains after the embalmers had finished with them. This initial phase would have entailed not only the structural design of the pyramid, but also selection of a suitable site for the structure and identification of rock formations within a reasonable distance of the site capable of supplying the bulk of the stone for the pyramid. Design changes took place during construction of most of the pyramids: the Step Pyramid was converted from a mastaba first into a four-step pyramid and finally into a six-step one; the Meidum Pyramid was converted from a seven- to an eight-step structure and, with disastrous consequences, saw the addition of an outer smoothing layer.

The pyramid builders were fortunate in having sites available where they could found these structures on good quality rock, able to bear their huge weight. In the one instance, at South Dahshur, where the underlying geological formation appears not to be hard rock but probably a stiff deformable clay, settlements in the foundations forced the builders to take measures to try and counteract all too obvious signs of distress in the tomb chambers and corridors and in the structure itself, eventually leading to the decision to finish the pyramid at a flatter angle and abandon it.

Having chosen the site, the outline of the pyramid base would have been marked out, carefully orienting the four sides to the cardinal points, which was achieved with great accuracy. The maximum misalignment in the Great Pyramid occurs in the east side, which bears less than one-tenth of a degree west of true north and, with the exception of the Step Pyramid and the Meidum Pyramid where there are misalignments of up to three degrees and approaching half a degree respectively, the maximum misalignments are less than one-quarter of a degree. The larger misalignments in the Step and Meidum Pyramids are explained in part by the changes in design implemented during construction, and in part by the surveyors still perfecting their techniques in these first two completed pyramids.

The north–south alignments of the east and west sides of the pyramid bases must have been fixed by celestial sightings, possibly based on sighting to a star in the northern heavens as suggested by Edwards. By observing from a fixed point the rising and setting positions of the star and bisecting the angle between these and the observation point the true north–south alignment is determined. As pointed out by Edwards, this requires a true

A method suggested by Edwards for establishing a true north–south line. O is the centre at ground level of a circular wall with a level top; P' and Q' are positions of the selected star in the east and west respectively; P and Q the corresponding points at the top of the wall; *p* and *q* the corresponding points at the base of the wall. ON is the north–south line found by bisecting the angle *qOp*.

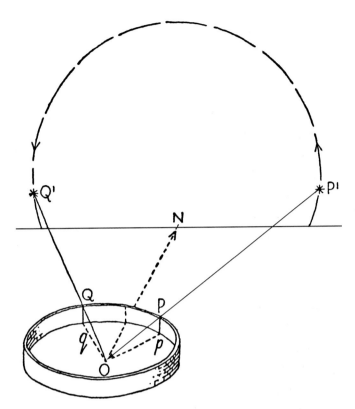

horizontal horizon, free of irregularities, which could have been achieved by building a circular wall with a level top at sufficient height to prevent the observer within the wall seeing anything outside except the sky. The horizontality could have been ensured by a water-filled groove in the top of the wall. An alternative method, proposed by Lehner, is based on observing two equal lengths of the sun's shadow cast by a vertical rod at different times and bisecting the angle between them.

Once fixed, the north–south alignment formed either the east or west side of the pyramid base. The remaining operations to establish the base sides required accurate measurements of length and a means of setting out the north and south sides exactly at right angles to the north–south alignment. Accurate linear measurements require the use of a 'standard' length which, for Egyptian building, took the form of a wooden 'cubit' rod, several of which have been found showing slight variations in length from 523mm to 529mm and averaging about 525mm. Seven palms made up one cubit and four digits one palm. Accurate measurements over large distances, such as fixing the length of the side of a pyramid, would have required the use of something longer than one-cubit rods and probably took the form of calibrated rods up to 10 cubits in length. Calibrated cords, perhaps 100 cubits in length with knots or loops marking the cubit divisions, would have been more convenient to use where absolute precision was not at a premium, such as in land measurement. In this context it is probably significant, as pointed out by Dieter Arnold, that the number 100 in hieroglyphs is represented by a rope.

Establishing a short straight line a metre or two at right angles to an existing straight line would have been a simple task using a wooden square very like a carpenter's square used today. Squares like this have been found. Extending such a line accurately to 200m or more would have been well nigh impossible, and some other technique is most likely to have been used. Despite Pythagorus still being some 2,000 years in the future, the ancient Egyptians probably knew of the 3,4,5 triangle, and, in the unlikely absence of this knowledge, could have used cords to draw intersecting arcs from two well-spaced points on the base line, connecting the intersection points of the arcs to mark out the right angle line.

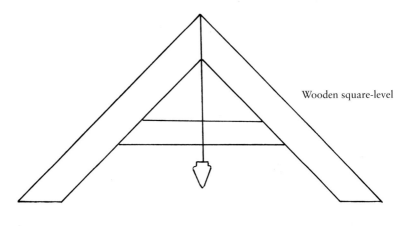

Wooden square-level

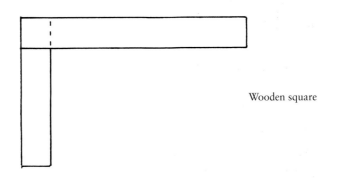

Wooden square

The Egyptian builders could have set out horizontal lines using a wooden square-level and right angles using a simple wooden square. Examples of these devices have been found. Right angles could also have been set out using intersecting arcs.

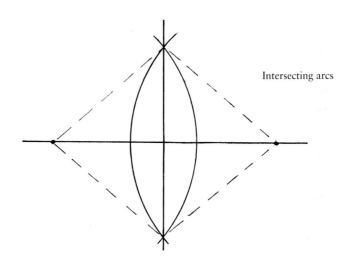

Intersecting arcs

67

The initial task of site preparation would have been the clearing away of loose and soft surface layers, followed by chipping away protuberances and high spots or areas of rock, sufficiently for the builders to establish a solid horizontal base with the first few layers of placed blocks. In the case of the Great Pyramid the entire perimeter was levelled to about 20mm, but a knoll of rock was left upstanding in the centre of the site to become incorporated into the structure. It has been suggested by Edwards that to achieve this degree of accuracy the Egyptians used their knowledge and experience in levelling fields for irrigation, completely surrounding the pyramid site with a low bank of Nile mud and filling the resulting enclosure with water. Trenches could then have been dug with floor levels at the same depth below water level and the intervening projections of rock removed after draining off the water.

Mark Lehner challenges this scenario on the basis that it would have been impossible to carry up to the Giza plateau the quantity of water required, using the only water-lifting technology of the time, namely simple shoulder poles with pots slung on the ends. He cites evaporation as an added problem. It is difficult to believe, however, that people capable of transporting the vast quantities of rock required for the pyramids could not have found a way of getting sufficient water to the site to perform a levelling operation as described by Edwards. More importantly, perhaps, Mark Lehner makes the point that the natural slope of the plateau meant that, in some locations, the rock level had to be cut down by as much as 10m to achieve a sufficiently level surface on which to place a base layer of stone, the surface of which would have been levelled precisely.

Horizontal lines can be established by making sightings at right angles to vertical plumb lines, and simple devices for doing this, called square-levels, have been discovered and are now displayed in the Cairo Museum. These are in the form of two straight lengths of wood connected at their ends to form a right angle, with a cross- piece at their mid-lengths to give an **A** shape; the free ends of the splayed pieces are at the same level when a suspended plumb line, secured at the apex, coincides with a carefully placed calibrated mark on the cross-piece. A horizontal sighting can be made along a long straight rod with a square-level attached to it. Field tests reported by Arnold showed that differences in height of about 10mm could be recognised with some difficulty for sighting distances up to 40 to 45m. It is possible that this accuracy could have been sufficient to establish levels within 20mm or so, as observed at Khufu's pyramid, by several traverses and traverse reversals.

SIX

Stone Sources and Quarrying

The Egyptian builders were fortunate in having a variety of hard and soft, igneous, metamorphic and sedimentary rocks available from which they could quarry their stone blocks to satisfy the functional demands of their structures or simply to meet the exacting requirements of their architects. They also had Nile mud from which, with the addition of straw, they made sun-dried bricks, far and away the most widely used building material in ancient Egypt, and which formed the basic building material for the numerous pyramids constructed after the close of the age of stone pyramids. The one material they lacked – good quality timber – they imported at considerable expense, mostly from Lebanon, and consequently used sparingly in building. Surviving fragments of the Palermo Stone, carved in the V Dynasty to record events in the reigns of preceding kings, make mention of the importation of forty shiploads of cedar wood in one year during the reign of Snofru. There may well have been many such shipments during his reign, much of which would have been used in ship building and pyramid construction. Egypt had its own trees, as seen in many wall illustrations, including acacia, sycamore and tamarisk used for lesser joinery and structural work, and also palm, the fibrous nature of which made it unsuitable for joinery work. It was used extensively for roofing. Herodotus states that acacia wood was used to make the hulls and masts of freight-carrying Nile boats, and tamarisk was used for rafts attached to these boats to catch the current and help propel the boats along.

The geological features seen in Egypt today emerged some 27 million years ago during the Miocene period, when a rise in the level of the land resulted in deep erosion by rapid flowing sea-bound waters, cutting down through formerly inundated deposits exposed by a retreating sea. The waters gouged out a gorge, generally 10 to 16km wide, which became partially filled with sands and gravels as the velocity of the sediment-laden waters slowed. The Nile established its bed in these deep deposits and has constantly changed its course; ground investigations at a site between Sohag and Asyut, for example, have shown that in historical times the river has migrated over 3km eastward across its floodplain.

The oldest and hardest rocks exposed by the eroding waters were the igneous granites and diorites in southern Egypt, which the Old Kingdom builders exploited, particularly the red and grey granites from Aswan, for their pyramid tomb chambers and, to a limited extent, for external cladding in the case of the Giza pyramids of Khafre and Menkaure (and the unfinished pyramid at Abu Roash). Some use was made of basalt, a dark igneous rock from the Fayum area, notably for pavements; the basalt paving of Khufu's temple at Giza still survives, although the rest of the temple has now disappeared.

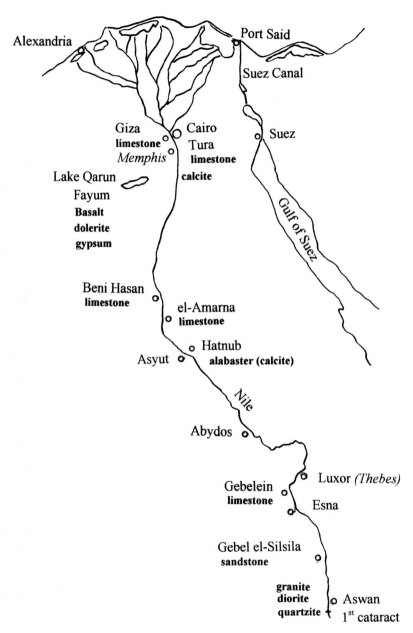

Mediterranean

Alexandria

Port Said

Suez Canal

Giza
limestone
Memphis

Cairo
Tura
limestone
calcite

Suez

Lake Qarun
Fayum
Basalt
dolerite
gypsum

Gulf of Suez

Beni Hasan
limestone

el-Amarna
limestone

Hatnub
alabaster (calcite)

Asyut

Nile

Abydos

Luxor *(Thebes)*

Gebelein
limestone

Esna

Gebel el-Silsila
sandstone

granite
diorite
quartzite

Aswan
1st cataract

Locations of rock types used for building construction in ancient Egypt.

Quartzite, a hard silicified or metamorphosed sandstone, also occurs in a number of locations in Egypt, particularly near Aswan, but Old Kingdom builders made no use of it.

The softer sedimentary rocks fringing the Nile valley are mostly limestones, extending some 600km south from Cairo to near Esna; but south of this almost to Aswan, and again beyond Aswan, the hills bordering the Nile are primarily of sandstone, a massive outcrop of the latter occurring, for example, at Gebel El Silsila. While nearly all the huge temples in Upper Egypt dating from the New Kingdom and later periods are built of sandstone, very little, if any, use was made of it during the Old Kingdom period. Alabaster was mined in a number of areas, notably Hatnub, from the III Dynasty onwards for use as a subsidiary building material for lining passages and rooms, its soft smooth texture making it very easy to work. The name alabaster is in fact a misnomer in this case: actually the Egyptians employed calcite, a compact crystalline form of calcium carbonate, not true alabaster which is a form of calcium sulphate. Two other water-deposited materials, Nile silt and gypsum from the Fayum area, provided the basic ingredients for mortar and plaster, used extensively in the construction of the pyramids and their associated structures.

Menes located his capital Memphis where he could most effectively exercise control over his unified realm; fortuitously he had also selected a site close to limestone deposits excellent for building purposes. At Saqqara, Dahshur and Giza the Old Kingdom builders exploited the local limestone, and the topography of the Giza plateau, as it appears today, has been formed largely by quarrying operations. The Mokattam limestone formation, from which the Giza plateau is formed, yields a distinctive rock containing large numbers of nummulite fossils, and it is this rock that makes up the bulk of the pyramid structures. Attesting to the quarrying activities on the Giza plateau are the various depressions pitting the surface, some sand filled, as well as the excavated area around the Sphinx and a ravenous bite taken out of the plateau some 300m south of the Great Pyramid, which, with a depth of as much as 30m, could alone have supplied much of the stone for Khufu's pyramid. Directly across the Nile at Tura and Masara the builders had access to a finer quality, fossil-free limestone that was used as outer casing for the stone pyramids.

Many of the limestone quarries yielding the blocks for the stone pyramids have been identified, and have provided evidence of the quarrying methods used. The tools available to the quarrymen for excavating the rock would have been picks and chisels of copper, the only metal known to have been used in the Old Kingdom, perhaps supplemented by hard stone tools on occasion; timber in various guises, together with ropes, would have been used in the freeing and subsequent handling of the stone blocks. Block sizes would have been dictated largely by quarry conditions, but the builders would have been well aware of the advantages of quarrying blocks as large as possible, compatible with the means adopted to transport them to the construction site and to raise and handle them into their final position. The larger the blocks, the less would be the amount of excavation and surface preparation required for the same volume of blocks produced. Increasing all the linear dimensions of a rectangular block by a quarter almost doubles the volume, but only increases the surface area by slightly more than a half.

The limestone exploited by the Old Kingdom builders was deposited in horizontal layers under the sea and, as now seen in cliff exposures, consists of good quality, or anyway adequate quality, layers of rock separated by distinct horizontal, or very nearly horizontal, bedding planes. As the layers provided blocks of suitable thickness for pyramid construction, and the bedding planes were planes of weakness allowing the blocks to be readily prised free of the underlying rock, the quarrying operations would have been relatively straightforward, despite the limitations in available tools. Where the depth of overburden and poor quality rock was not great, limestone blocks would have been obtained by quarrying cliff faces, working the faces back in a series of open steps. Blocks were separated from the parent rock by vertical trenches, probably dug out mostly by picks, but chisels may have been needed in awkward places. The widths of blocks for the Great Pyramid, generally between 0.5m and 1.5m, and averaging about 0.8m, would have been influenced by the distance between bedding planes, in order to obtain blocks of satisfactory cross-section, either square or very nearly so. Similarly, trench widths would have been dictated by their depth, shallow trenches less than 1m in depth having a width of about 300mm or less, but deeper trenches needing to be wider to allow free access. After completion of the trenches, separation of a block from the underlying rock could have been effected by hammering in copper wedges at the base, or by using levers, either inserted into slots cut around the base of the block and freeing it with a lifting motion or, more likely, by inserting the levers into the top of the trench on one side and exerting a sideways force near the top of the block to tilt it, and so break the weak bonding across the bedding plane at the base of the block.

Exposed limestone cliff face near the Giza pyramids showing clearly the bedding planes. These would have allowed blocks to be easily prised from the underlying rock.

Engineering the Pyramids

Limestone quarries could have been worked in a number of different ways, depending to some extent on detailed geological characteristics of the particular limestone deposit. One possible solution for open face quarries would have been to work the face in sections, each perhaps six steps in height and twenty block widths in length. Assuming blocks 0.8m square in section and trench widths 0.3m, the sections would have been 4.8m high and 22m long. For convenience of working, step widths would need to have been equal to at least three block lengths, or about 5.4m, assuming block lengths to be twice their width and trenches 0.3m wide. This would have given the quarrymen adequate working space, and would have allowed the blocks to be conveyed along the steps to gently sloping ramps cut into the rock at the ends of the sections, along which the blocks would have been raised or lowered to plateau level, depending on the relative levels of the quarry and plateau. With three-block step widths the ramp slopes would have been about 1 in 7.

The sections would have been worked from both ends, employing perhaps six men for each group of three blocks. Once a block was prised free from its parent rock and given at least a preliminary dressing, it would have been handed over to a transport gang, who would have conveyed the block to the construction site.

Some idea of the quarry size can be obtained by accepting the generally quoted figure that the Great Pyramid consists of 2.3 million blocks, placed within the 23-year reign of Pharaoh Khufu, implying a placement rate, on average, of about 300 a day or one every two minutes throughout the entire construction period. If each three blocks took two days to produce, each quarry section would have produced 36 blocks every two days, and consequently the production of 300

Stump remains of limestone blocks removed from the quarry sited just to the north of the Khafre Pyramid. (D. Wildung)

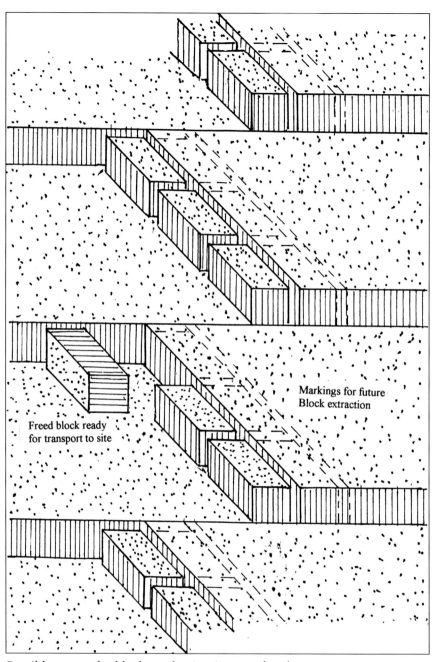

Markings for future
Block extraction

Freed block ready
for transport to site

Possible system for block production in open-face limestone quarrying.

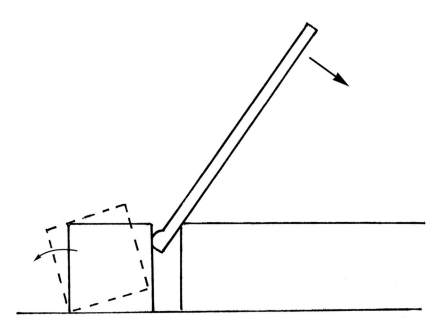

Prising a limestone block free of underlying rock.

blocks a day would have required the working of seventeen sections simultaneously, giving a total length of quarry face being worked at any one time, for average production, of about 425m, assuming block widths of 0.8m, trench widths of 0.3m and ramp widths of 3m. Peak production would have been achieved by working more steps, greater single quarry face lengths, or more than one quarry.

The manpower employed in quarrying can be estimated by assuming that each six-man quarry gang produced three blocks every two days. The six men would have been variously engaged in trenching, sharpening tools, clearing away waste and other ancillary tasks, and finally levering the blocks free of the underlying parent rock, followed by any dressing or shaping of

Entrances to underground quarry galleries at Tura (in upper part of photograph) viewed from a distance.

the blocks to be done at the quarry. This gives an estimate of 1,200 men working the limestone quarries at any particular time to produce the average required output of 300 blocks a day. Allowing for the cutting of ramps and the removal of overburden in open face quarrying, and much slower production from the underground Tura galleries, a more realistic number to achieve average output might be up to 1,500 men. As one of the tasks of the NOVA project, to build a diminutive pyramid near the Giza plateau, carried out under the direction of archaeologist Mark Lehner and stonemason Roger Hopkins a few years ago, 12 quarrymen produced 186 blocks in 22 working days, leading to a figure of 1,212 for the quarry workforce for Khufu's pyramid, with the rider that the actual number would have been higher, as the NOVA workmen used iron tools and a winch to extract the stones. Thus the estimate of 1,500 is not in serious dispute with the NOVA figure.

The actual workforce in the quarries must, at times of peak production, have greatly exceeded 1,500, because in order to achieve an average placement rate of 300 blocks a day, a much faster placement rate would have been needed in placing the lower courses to compensate for the inevitable slowing of the rate as the height of the pyramid increased. There would have been no possibility of earlier stockpiling, as the volume of the three pyramids attributed to Snofru, who reigned for 26 years and thus barely longer than Khufu, exceeded the volume of the Great Pyramid by 40 per cent. The frenetic activity continued after Khufu for the construction of the pyramid of Khafre. Peak production from the limestone quarries must have been at least 50 per cent higher than average, and possibly double the average.

Construction of the pyramids required outstanding organisational skills, not only to get the maximum efficiency

Found in a closed room (serdab) on the north side of his Step Pyramid, this statue of Pharaoh Djoser in the Cairo Museum is the earliest large stone royal statue found in Egypt. It shows Djoser in the costume worn by monarchs for the sed *festival, a ritual performed at intervals of several years to demonstrate the king's renewed physical strength and spiritual powers. A retinue of priests and dignitaries would view the king performing various physical feats such as archery and footrunning.* (Ancient Egypt Picture Library)

This limestone stela in the Cairo Museum, found in the subsidiary pyramid of the South Dahshur (Bent) Pyramid, depicts Snofru, the first pharaoh of the IV Dynasty, to whom three of the seven stone pyramids are attributed – Meidum, South Dahshur and North Dahshur. The Meidum Pyramid may originally have been intended for his predecessor and father, Huni, about whom little is known. A much smaller step pyramid at Seila, 10km west of Meidum, is also attributed to Snofru. As the structural collapse at Meidum and the settlement problems at South Dahshur rendered both of these structures unsuitable for the body of the god-king, the North Dahshur Pyramid had to be completed quickly and with structural integrity, both of these factors no doubt influencing the decision to use the flatter slopes for its construction. (Ancient Egypt Picture Library)

Only about 130mm high, this ivory statuette in the Cairo Museum is the only known surviving figure of Khufu, a pharaoh much reviled by Herodotus, who was merely repeating the biased accounts of the Egyptian priests of his own time, some 2,000 years after the pyramid age. There is no evidence that he closed the temples as claimed by the priests (he may have been confused with Akhnaten) or that Egyptians were forced to labour as slaves on the construction of the Great Pyramid for Khufu. The latter belief may have stemmed from the monumental effort which would have been required to build the Great Pyramid; but, ironically, his father, Snofru, was greatly revered throughout pharaonic times, despite the fact that three major stone pyramids are attributed to him, having a total volume 40 per cent greater than that of Khufu's pyramid. (AKG London/Erich Lessing)

This diorite statue of Khafre, for whom the second Giza pyramid was constructed, shows him wearing the royal beard and headdress. He is protected by the spread wings of the Horus falcon, perched on the high-backed throne on which Khafre is seated. The statue, in the Cairo Museum, projects both the dignity and supreme power of the pharaoh. However, he fares little better than his father Khufu in the accounts of the later priests as recorded by Herodotus, perhaps reflecting the fact that the size of his pyramid, and consequently the task of constructing it, was only slightly less than that of the Great Pyramid. (AKG London/François Guénet)

One of a number of surviving group statues of Menkaure, for whom the third and
smallest Giza pyramid was built. In this statue in the Cairo Museum he is shown
flanked by the goddess Hathor and a local nome (district) goddess. Menkaure died
before completion of his pyramid and it was finished by his son and successor,
Shepseskhaf, who contented himself with a large mudbrick mastaba at South
Saqqara, thus bringing to an end the age of stone pyramid building. In their
accounts to Herodotus the priests were much more kindly disposed towards
Menkaure than to his father Khafre and grandfather Khufu, no doubt reflecting the
much smaller effort that would have been required in the construction of his
pyramid, which had a volume less than one-tenth that of the Great Pyramid. (AKG
London/François Guénet)

In extending Djoser's intended mastaba into a six-step pyramid, Imhotep initiated some 160 years of frenetic stone pyramid construction in Egypt. Administrator and scribe, sage and writer, engineer-architect and healer of the sick, his reputation grew with the telling throughout pharaonic times. Deified by later generations of Egyptians, and by the Greeks, he is shown here in a sixth-century BC bronze sculpture as a seated priest holding an unrolled papyrus scroll on his knees. The sculpture is now in the British Museum. (R. Sheridan/Ancient Art & Architecture Collection)

The corbelled roof of this antechamber of the North Dahshur Pyramid is technically more sophisticated than those in the earlier pyramids at Meidum and South Dahshur. (AKG London/François Guénet)

A scene from the Middle Kingdom tomb of Ity at Gebelein, south of Luxor, illustrating the use of donkeys to transport grain to a granary, with human labour taking over to fill the grain stores. Domesticated antelopes are also shown. The scene is now in the Museo Egizio, Turin. (AKG London/Nimatallah)

Shadufs are still used today to raise water for irrigation. (AKG London/Erich Lessing)

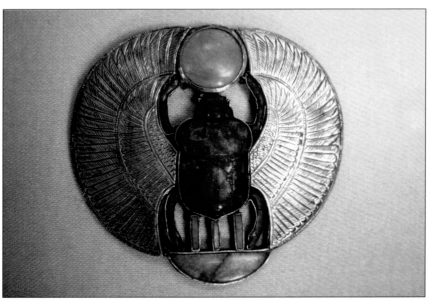

Were the ancient Egyptians inspired to roll the pyramid blocks by watching the sacred scarab beetle rolling its dung ball, often several times the weight of the beetle itself? Having formed the dung ball, the beetle propelled it along until it dropped into a convenient hole in the ground, where it served as food for its young emerging family. In Egyptian theology the beetle depicted life itself, sometimes laying its eggs in the bodies of dead beetles, thus projecting an image of resurrection as the young beetles emerged. It was also a sacred beetle which pushed the sun into the Other World in the evening, but unfailingly rolled it back over the horizon to reappear each morning. (Ancient Egypt Picture Library)

from the men at work, but also to accommodate them and supply them with food, water and tools. No doubt the scribes kept a careful record of these supplies. Herodotus gives an account of an inscription on the Great Pyramid recording an amount of 1,500 talents spent on radishes, onions and leeks for the labourers and reflects on how much must have been spent in addition on bread and clothing for them.

Every available daylight hour must have been exploited to complete these gargantuan structures over such short periods of time, and this was achieved by rotating the workforce every three or four months; this presumably also kept to acceptable levels the adverse effect of the drain on the workforce required for agricultural production. The men worked nine days at a stretch with every tenth day off, allowing them some respite from the daily toil and the opportunity to visit their families if these lived near enough or to carry out some chores, such as mending or washing clothes. Excavations of workmen's sites near the Giza pyramids have revealed the remains of mudbrick workshops, storehouses and huts, the last each housing a dozen workers and containing a kitchen, cellar and an oven for baking bread.

At Tura, on the eastern side of the Nile, it was necessary to make underground galleries to access the formations of fine quality limestone used for the outer casing blocks of the pyramids. As this is now a military area the openings to the galleries have to be viewed from a distance, making them seem rather insignificant; in fact, they are up to 6m high, giving access to galleries penetrating hundreds of metres or even kilometres into the mountain, with a forest of supporting pillars disappearing into the distance until lost in the darkness.

The techniques of hard rock quarrying were in many respects different from, and much more arduous than, those

Limestone in a quarry near Tura.

for soft rock. Copper saws, combined with a very hard grit such as emery, may have been used to a limited extent, but for the most part hand-operated stone pounders were employed, many of which, probably dating from the New Kingdom, have been found in the granite quarries at Aswan. It has been estimated that granite consumption from Aswan in the Old Kingdom for pyramid and temple construction amounted to some 45,000 cubic metres, much of this from large, naturally occurring boulders. These were shaped and dressed using pear-shaped dolerite pounders, 4 to 7kg in weight, held in both hands at the broad end and striking the rock repeatedly with the narrower end. Such pounders would have had a limited life and been discarded once they had aquired a roughly spherical shape. The much less arduous technique of heating and quenching would almost certainly have also seen extensive use, particularly in the preliminary shaping of blocks.

It may have been necessary to quarry the larger granite beams from the living rock, such as those spanning the roof of the King's Chamber in the Great Pyramid, and the techniques evident in the famous unfinished obelisk at Aswan, of New Kingdom age and so dating from a thousand years later, may well have been used. Each block was trenched all round in sections, each of sufficient length to accommodate a squatting or kneeling worker pounding the stone, and partially undercut at its base to weaken it sufficiently to be freed from

Opposite: The unfinished obelisk at Aswan of New Kingdom age, probably abandoned because of cracking in the rock. It is believed that the trenches isolating the obelisk from the parent rock were excavated by pounding the granite with hard dolerite balls, a method probably used 1,000 years earlier at Aswan to excavate some of the larger granite beams for the King's Chamber in the Great Pyramid.

the underlying rock by tilting the block using huge levers inserted into the trenches and reacting against the adjacent intact rock. Once released from the parent rock, the beam would have been largely shaped to its final form at the quarry site to facilitate its handling and transportation. It then had to be loaded on to special boats made from Lebanese cedar. Under the command of a watchful pilot, familiar with the shifting sandbanks which still bedevil the course of tourist boats today, the beam would be floated with the current down the Nile, reaching its offloading point for the Giza plateau in about one week.

SEVEN

Herodotus on Pyramid Construction

The best description of how the Great Pyramid was built is still that by Herodotus, the Greek historian and 'Father of History'. Although he wrote some two millennia after the great pyramid age, he had the advantage of discussions with Egyptian priests and learned people, whose professions may well have retained some memories and, indeed, some of the techniques, of those earlier times.

Born around 480 BC, Herodotus lived and wrote at the time of the Golden Age of Athens, although not himself an Athenian. He was the son of a well-respected family living in Halicarnassus (now Bodrun in south-west Turkey), a Greek city-state at that time under the control of the powerful Persian Empire. Leaving Halicarnassus as a young man, he travelled extensively in the Greek and Persian world, clearly making copious notes of his own observations and things he was told, some factual and some nothing more than tall tales. Much attracted to Athens, he visited that city several times and took up residence there in 447 BC, remaining about four years before finally moving to Thurii, a recently established

Athenian colony in the instep of the Italian boot. He died there between 425 and 430 BC. The anecdotal nature of his writing, and the inclusion of amusing and diverting tales which are clearly nonsense, probably reflects the fact that his original presentations, made orally, were designed to hold the attention of an audience.

His writings on Egypt, then under the control of Persia with a Persian pharaoh, are particularly percipient. Having observed, for example, (sea) shells on the hills fringing the Nile valley, he theorises correctly that Egypt had once been an arm of the sea. He also gives an account of the ancient Suez Canal connecting an arm of the Nile to the Red Sea. His description of the building of the Great Pyramid is worth quoting in full here, in Aubrey de Selincourt's translation, revised by A.R. Burn in 1972.

> Up to the time of Rhampsinitus [Snofru], Egypt was excellently governed and very prosperous; but his successor Cheops (continuing the account which the priests gave me) brought the country into all sorts of misery. He closed all the temples, then, not content with excluding his subjects from the practice of their religion, compelled them without exception to labour as slaves for his own advantage. Some were forced to drag blocks of stone from the quarries in the Arabian hills to the Nile, where they were ferried across and taken over by others, who hauled them to the Libyan hills. The work went on in three monthly shifts, a hundred thousand men in a shift. It took ten years of this oppressive slave labour to build the track along which the blocks were hauled – a work, in my opinion, of hardly less magnitude than the pyramid itself, for it is five furlongs in length, sixty feet wide, forty-eight feet high at its highest point, and constructed of polished stone blocks decorated with carvings of animals. To build it took, as I said,

ten years – including the underground sepulchral chambers on the hill where the pyramid stands; a cut was made from the Nile, so that the water from it turned the site of these into an island. To build the pyramid itself took twenty years; it is square at the base, its height (800ft) equal to the length of each side; it is of polished stone blocks beautifully fitted, none of the blocks being less than thirty feet long. The method employed was to build it in steps, or, as some call them, tiers or terraces. When the base was complete, the blocks for the first tier above it were lifted from ground level by contrivances made of short timbers; on this first tier there was another, which raised the blocks a stage higher, then another which raised them higher still. Each tier, or storey, had its set of levers, or it may be that they used the same one, which, being easy to carry, they shifted up from stage to stage as soon as its load was dropped into place. Both methods are mentioned, so I give them both here. The finishing-off of the pyramid was begun at the top and continued downwards, ending with the lowest parts nearest the ground.

It is immediately obvious from this account that Cheops (Khufu) was getting a bad press among the priests during Herodotus' time in Egypt, their criticism possibly intended to ingratiate them with their Persian masters. Today it is not thought by Egyptologists that Khufu was a tyrant or that he forced the workmen to labour as slaves, although much of the work must unquestionably have been arduous.

It is not always clear exactly what Herodotus is saying and some of the numbers are clearly wrong, suggesting that this passage, and probably much of Herodotus' work, has suffered from earlier imprecise rewrites, transcriptions and translations. His claim that none of the stones was less than 30ft long is wrong by a factor of ten, suggesting either that an error has crept into earlier translations or that the pyramid was in a pristine, smooth faced, condition when he visited it and he could not see individual blocks. His base length of 800ft is about 6 per cent too long, but the actual height of 147m (481ft) is certainly not equal to the base length of 230m (755ft), a mistake which indicates that his was probably only a visual assessment, and that he was fooled by the imposing appearance of the structure. Interestingly, if he had climbed the pyramid and the smoothed facing blocks were still intact, he could not have climbed directly up the 52 degree slope of the face, but probably could have clambered up the lesser 42 degree slope of one of the corners; if at the same time he had measured the corner length he would have found it almost the same as the base length. Is this what he meant by the height?

Unlike some modern writers presenting their views on the building of the pyramids, Herodotus clearly realised that transporting the blocks from the quarries to the site was a task matching that of the actual pyramid construction. He obviously knew from his discussions with the priests that some of the blocks came from the 'Arabian hills' (Tura) on the other side of the Nile, a monumental transportation task in itself. He also makes much of the task of building a track 5 furlongs (about 1km) in length, along which to haul the blocks, presumably from the local quarry, but possibly the last stage in hauling the blocks from Tura. A period of ten years to build this road is surely too long as it would have held up pyramid construction, and the figure of 100,000 men a shift, working in three monthly shifts, to build it is certainly too high and may have been a number he conjured up to impress on his audience the magnitude of the task of building the road. Whenever the Great Pyramid is mentioned by modern writers, it is invariably stated that Herodotus said it took 100,000 men twenty years to build it; in fact this number relates directly to the haul road and Herodotus does not specifically offer a number for building the pyramid. Of course, it may be inferred that he had the same number in mind.

It is now generally accepted that the Great Pyramid was built up in steps or tiers as stated by Herodotus, but this was probably not the case with the earliest pyramids with their buttress wall construction. Perhaps the most important statement in this account is that the stones were raised by means of contrivances made of short timbers. A number of writers have proposed that the stones were raised by levers and have used this description to support their contention. In fact, Herodotus' account suggests quite the opposite: a lever must be a single long, or very long, piece of timber to be effective. Where Herodotus wants to convey the fact that levers were used he says so explicitly later in the account, and there is no doubt he is correct that they were used to manoeuvre the blocks into their final position after they had been dropped close to it, and no doubt the levers were, as he says, moved up from stage to stage. The statement 'on this first tier there was another, which raised the blocks a stage higher, then yet another which raised them higher still' has often been interpreted to imply 'another contrivance', but the previous reference to contrivances is in the plural. In fact another almost certainly refers to another tier. Finally by the 'finishing-off' of the pyramid, beginning at the top, Herodotus presumably means the chipping away of the outer steps to achieve a smooth surface.

EIGHT

Levers, Rockers and Cranes

Methods which have been proposed in the literature for raising the stones to build the pyramids may be broadly divided into two categories: those that require ramps, and those that do not. The former category includes the proposed use of levers, rockers and various forms of primitive crane.

While much use would certainly have been made of levers in the quarrying, transport and pyramid construction operations, it is unlikely that they were involved in the major operation of raising the stones, although a number of writers have proposed their use for just this purpose. In fact, their involvement is likely to have been confined to prising blocks free from the parent rock in the quarry, preparing and/or loading blocks for transportation to the construction site, manoeuvring blocks during transportation and their final positioning once they had been transported to within a few centimetres of their ultimate destination on the working platform.

Although complicated access arrangements have been suggested for raising the stones by levers, such as cantilevered courses and stairways, the only practicable approach would

Levers, Rockers and Cranes

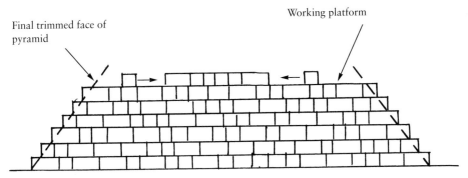

Pyramid construction entailed not just the raising of the stones, but transportation of the stones from the quarries to the site and, after raising the stones, moving them for distances of up to 100m across the working platform to their final position. (Not to scale)

have been to utilise the outer steps formed by the coursed method of construction adopted for the North Dahshur Pyramid and all later stone pyramids, including the Great Pyramid. The narrowness of the steps presents a problem in any attempt to promote this as a possible method of raising the stones; as shown by Petrie, the course thicknesses in the Great Pyramid are not constant, generally ranging from about 1.5m at the base to 0.5m approaching the top, but fluctuating through the height of the structure rather than showing a progressive decrease. The average step height is about 0.75m. As the pyramid slope angle is 52° the step widths range from about 1.2m to 0.4m, with an average width of about 0.6m. Assuming each course was completed before starting the next one, it follows that these are the widths on which the men wielding the levers would have had to stand. It is possible to lift a block by alternative levering from each end, or by levering from one end only inserting a progressively higher

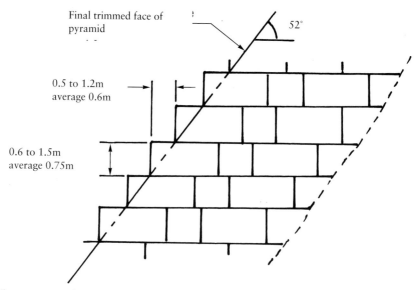

Final trimmed face of pyramid

52°

0.5 to 1.2m
average 0.6m

0.6 to 1.5m
average 0.75m

The steps on the outer faces of the Great Pyramid may have been utilised in raising the stones, but are very narrow, often narrower than the widths of the blocks being raised.

central support. Lifting a 2.5 tonne block would have required at least two men standing side by side at one or both ends, but it would have been impossible for two men to stand side by side on steps with such small widths. The widths of the blocks being lifted would often have been greater than the step widths, making the operation additionally hazardous, particularly under a broiling hot desert sun or in howling wind, with the slightest slip meaning almost certain death or slippage of the stone, allowing it to tumble out of control down the face of the pyramid.

An even greater problem than the simple lifting of the stones would have arisen at the completion of each individual lift, when the stone had to be moved laterally on to the step above:

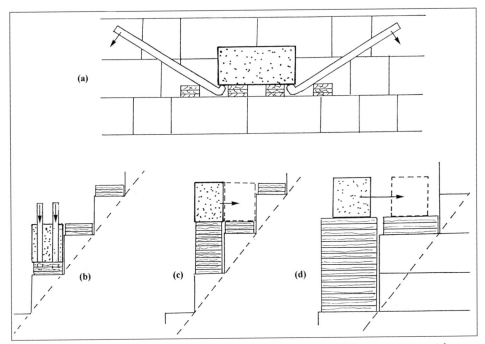

Although blocks can be raised by levering, the narrowness of the outer pyramid steps would have made levering up the blocks (a, b) virtually impossible. Moving the blocks sideways at the top of the lift posed another extremely hazardous problem. Doubling the size of steps (c, d) would have meant doubling the height of lift and the distance to be moved laterally. Even if a possible levering method could have been devised, it would have been too slow and did not provide a solution for transporting the stones from the quarries or across the working platform.

this could only have been achieved by swivelling the levers horizontally outwards away from the pyramid face, thus rotating the levers about their fulcrums, giving inward motions to their tips. Even supposing the men could have worked on these very narrow ledges, they would have had to lean out dangerously into space to impart a useful amount of movement in this way. The step widths could have been

Lifting a 2.5 tonne concrete block, equal to the average limestone block in the Great Pyramid, by levering at one end. Levering of blocks would clearly not be feasible on a step 0.5m wide, high up on the face of a pyramid.

increased by having step heights of two or three layers, but this would have increased both the lift height and the required lateral movement at the top of the lift, making the operation even more hazardous. It would also have greatly increased the amount of stone to be chipped away at the end of construction to achieve a smooth pyramid face.

Even if the stones could have been raised on to the working platform by levering, the problem still remained of how to move the stones across the platform, in some cases 100m or more, to their designated final position. This could not have been done by levering, and consequently the builders would

When excavating the New Kingdom mortuary temple of Queen Hatshepsut, Petrie found, in the foundation deposits, models of tools used in its construction, including wooden cradle-like devices, originals of which he believed could have been used in the construction of the pyramids. The example shown here is in the Cairo Museum.

have had to resort to some other method, such as placing the stones on rollers.

In common with all proposed methods that do not require ramps, raising the blocks by levering would have been too slow to satisfy the demanding logistics of placing a stone every two minutes. Some other method would have been required to transport the blocks from the quarry to the site, and across the working platform, which, in itself, might have been a more satisfactory way of raising the blocks using ramps.

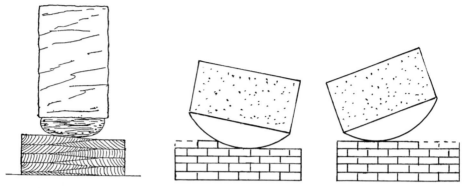

Petrie believed the cradle-like devices could have been used as rockers to raise the stones. Even if feasible on the narrow steps, it would have been a very dangerous operation.

While excavating foundation deposits in the mortuary temple of Queen Hatshepsut, near Luxor, Petrie came across models of tools used in the construction of the building. These included models of wooden cradle-like devices, which, although dating from the New Kingdom period and thus post-dating the Old Kingdom period by a thousand years, Petrie believed could have been used in the construction of the stone pyramids. He suggested that by mounting the blocks upright on prototypes of these models, the stones could have been raised by rocking them backwards and forwards and inserting a piece of wood each time under the rising end of the 'rocker'. Although this idea has been taken up and elaborated upon by others, it suffers from all the disadvantages of using levers to lift the stones, but would have been even more dangerous and difficult to control and did not, in itself, provide a method for moving the blocks laterally at the top of their lift. As pointed out by Arnold, it would have been extremely hazardous, if not impossible, to have manipulated such rocker-mounted blocks

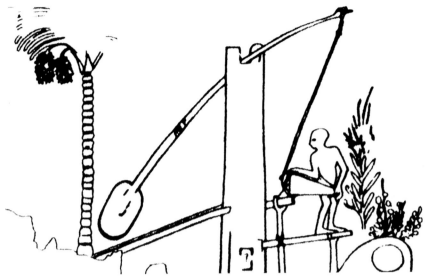

This view from a tomb in Thebes, dated around 1500 BC, shows a man who, having lifted water by means of a shaduf from a pool fringed by water plants, is pouring it into a sloping channel to conduct it to the base of a palm tree. Widely used in ancient times throughout Egypt and the Levant, the simple principle of the shaduf consisted of a balanced beam having a weight – often just a lump of clay – at one end of the beam to counter the weight of the water-filled container.

on the narrow outer steps of the pyramid structure, and the loss of control could have led to the working teams below being wiped out. However, the strongest argument against the 'rocking' proposal is that these cradle-like devices could have been used in a much more efficient and universal manner, not just for raising the stones, but also for their transportation from the quarries (see Chapter 10).

Primitive cranes have been advanced as a possible means of raising the pyramid stones, with at least one suggestion based on the shaduf, a device used by Egyptians in ancient times, and

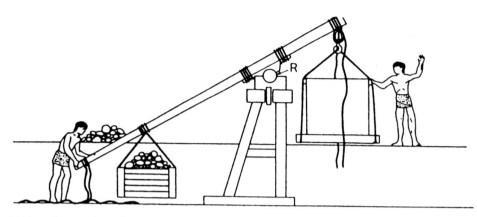

Lifting devices based on the balanced beam principle of the shaduf as shown here, and primitive cranes, have been proposed as a means of raising the pyramid stones, but they would have been too slow and cumbersome, not to say dangerous, for lifting stones weighing many tonnes. This example was proposed by J.P. Adam and modified by J. Kerisel to allow the beam to rotate about a vertical axis.

even today, to raise water from one level to a higher level, such as from a river or canal into an irrigation channel. The shaduf consists of a long balanced beam pivoted on top of an upright timber frame, often consisting simply of two posts and a cross-piece; a vertical rope attached to a water container is fixed to one end of the beam and is counterbalanced at the other end by a large stone or a wodge of dried clay. By hauling on the rope the operator lowers the water container into the river or canal until it is filled, then with minimum effort raises the counterbalanced filled container and empties it into the irrigation channel. It is a slow and tedious process, and even if devices based on the same principle could have been built capable of supporting stones several tonnes in weight, which is unlikely, they too could not have met the demanding logistics of placing a block every two minutes.

NINE

Sleds

There is a strong body of opinion among Egyptologists that sleds (or sledges; the words are interchangeable) were used to raise the pyramid stones, this method having the added advantage that it provided the means for transporting them from the quarries to the site and for moving the stones across the working platform. Although there are no physical remains dating from the Old Kingdom period, there is indisputable evidence that the ancient Egyptians knew of and used sleds. A notable example of a surviving sled now in the Cairo Museum was found buried near the Middle Kingdom pyramid of Senwosret III at Dahshur. It is 4.2m long and its two runners, 120mm by 200mm in section, are connected by four crossbeams with tongue and groove attachments. Only two other sleds, both smaller than this, have been found in Egypt.

The strong conviction that sleds were used in the construction of the pyramids has been largely engendered by the ubiquitous reproduction in texts on ancient Egypt, of a

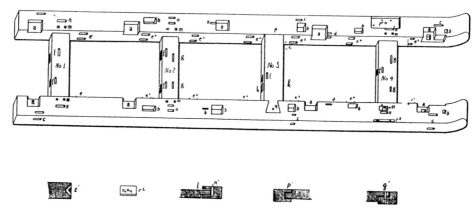

This sled, 4.2m long and 0.8m wide, found near the mudbrick pyramid of XII Dynasty pharaoh Senwroset III at Dahshur and dating from about 1840 BC, was used to haul boats to the pyramid site. The wooden boats and the sled were excavated in 1894 from shallow pits sunk into the sand. (*Reisner*)

striking wall illustration showing the transport of a huge alabaster statue of the XII Dynasty nomarch Djehutihotpe some 15km from the quarries at Hatnub to his capital of Hermopolis. The illustration on the walls of his tomb at Deir el-Bersheh shows 172 men hauling the statue which, as depicted, appears to be over 6m in height and probably weighed around 60 tonnes. In fact the size of the statue may have been exaggerated to enhance the image of its subject, as it is unlikely that the number of men shown could have hauled a statue of this size. Various attendants are shown accompanying the statue on its journey, including one man pouring what appears to be a lubricating liquid, perhaps water or olive oil, on to the ground in front of the sled. Three men are shown carrying additional supplies of the liquid and other groups of three carry a baulk of timber and short timber rods

The Dahshur sled in the
Cairo Museum. One of
the cross-pieces is
incorrectly attached.
(*Ancient Egypt Picture
Library*)

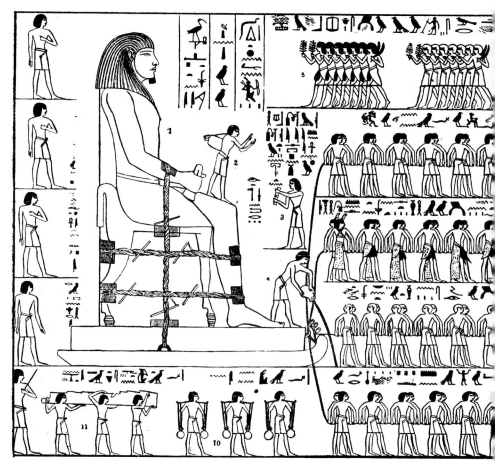

This famous tomb illustration (touched up from the damaged original) shows 172 men transporting by sledge the 60 tonne alabaster statue of XII Dynasty nomarch Djehutihotpe. As a one-off operation, intended as an impressive spectacle, it was very different to the transporting of pyramid stones, where speed was all important. The number of men actually required to haul this statue would have been considerably in excess of the number shown.

which may be levers, although rather ineffectual ones if really this length. The making of offerings and the burning of incense normally accompanied the transporting of important monuments, together with rhythmic chanting; a man standing on the knee of the statue can be seen leading the chanting to

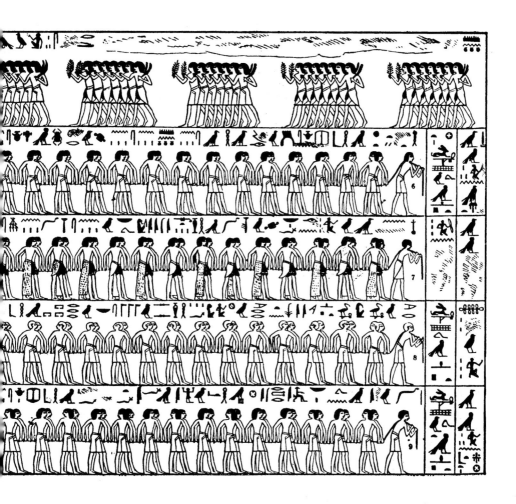

the beat of clackers played by a man standing just below him and facing him.

The circumstances behind the transportation of this statue differed greatly from those behind the transporting and raising of the pyramid stones. It was a one-off, deliberately intended by Djehutihotpe to provide a great spectacle, and the more men he had pulling it the more his image was enhanced. And to ensure the spectacle lasted as long as possible there would have been no exhortations to the 172 men to hurry it up. In an

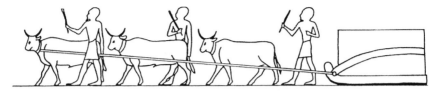

New Kingdom relief at Tura showing transportation of large block or sarcophagus using oxen.

inscription accompanying the wall illustration Djehutihotpe made it clear that to him belonged the credit for envisaging and successfully planning this exercise, but he did not stint his praise for those who carried it out. His eulogy included: 'I had young men come, the relief team of the recruits, to construct a road for the statue, as well as teams of quarrymen, administrators and specialists. The strong people said, "We can do it", and my heart rejoiced. The city assembled and let out cries of joy. The spectacle was more beautiful than anything.' Clearly it gladdened his politician's heart and served to make his loyal subjects forget their grievances, at least for the moment.

Another well-known illustration of sled usage is a New Kingdom relief from the Tura quarries showing the transportation of a large block pulled by oxen. As the oxen are out of proportion to their human handlers, it is difficult to assess the size of the block and consequently its purpose. It might even have been intended as a sarcophagus. It is generally believed that human power, rather than animal power, was used to transport and raise the pyramid stones.

Viewed from the perspective of elementary engineering mechanics, sleds represent a highly inefficient means of transportation, primarily because of the friction generated between the runners and the surface over which the sled is being moved. Proponents of the use of sleds have come up with various suggestions for how the friction may have been reduced, none of which is likely to have been practicable for transporting and raising the stones for the Great Pyramid and its immediate predecessors and successors, having in mind the requirement to place one stone every two minutes on average and with peak rates probably one every minute. This meant having a hundred or more stones in transit from the quarries to the site at any one time, and extracting stones simultaneously from hundreds of metres of quarry face. The sleds could not have been hauled over an untreated sand surface as they would have sunk into it, or over an untreated stone surface which would have generated a high frictional resistance and also would have rapidly worn down the sled runners. Clarke and Engelbach, referring to the floors of the exit passages at the Gebel El Silsila sandstone quarries, make the observation that 'they are quite rough and there are no indications that they had been prepared for sleds'.

Nile mud has been suggested as a means of reducing the friction, but can be discounted for a number of reasons. Quite apart from the vast amount that would have been required, if too soft the sleds would have sunk through it and even if stiff enough to be effective, it would not have greatly reduced the friction. Laboratory tests carried out in France by Jean Kerisel have shown that while the coefficient of friction of Nile mud is only about 0.12 under a low imposed pressure of 1 tonne per square metre, it rises rapidly with increasing pressure, becoming as high as 0.25 under 3 tonnes

Bas-relief at Kujundschik depicting Assyrians transporting a huge sled-mounted man-headed bull. Note the timber pieces placed under the sledge to give a timber-

on-timber sliding surface. The orientation of the timber pieces shows they were not being used as rollers.

per square metre. Under the hot desert sun and in the strong winds, it would have been well nigh impossible to have kept moist the areas of mud required, and drying mud would have acted as a binder rather than a lubricant. The use of any form of animal fat instead of mud can be dismissed, as the vast amount required would have ruined the pastoral economy, probably already under pressure as much of the corvée labour demands to construct the pyramids would have fallen on the rural population.

Another popular suggestion for reducing friction is the placing of rollers between the sled runners and the surface over which it is being drawn. This suggestion comes mostly from people who haven't tried it. For this system to work at all the underlying surface must be very firm and level, the rollers must be identical in size and of uniform diameter throughout their length or they will be prone to bunching up and snagging against each other, or possibly slewing around making the sled uncontrollable. The problems of controlling the rollers become even greater on a sloping gradient such as the slopes that had to be negotiated to extract the stones from the quarry faces or over the ramps to raise the stones in constructing the pyramids. The use of rollers in some circumstances cannot be entirely discounted, but could only be seriously contemplated for moving heavy objects short distances (up to a kilometre or so) over an unyielding level surface.

The only practicable surface over which sleds could have been drawn would have consisted of wood in some form, perhaps in a configuration rather like railway sleepers. The Assyrians in the eighth century BC were aware of this, as illustrated in a bas-relief at Kujundschik, excavated by Layard, showing the transportation of a sled-mounted gigantic statue of a man-headed bull. In what is manifestly a slow, laborious process, the statue is being drawn along by a large number of men pulling on ropes attached to both the front and rear of the sled, assisted by men hauling on an enormous lever at the rear. The presence of carts laden with spare ropes suggests that either the ropes had a short life or there existed a difficulty in assessing how many ropes and men would be required over some parts of the route. Most notably, the artist has shown lengths of timber under the sled, over which it is being drawn; men positioned in front of the sled are placing more timbers from a ready supply lying on the ground behind them. It is clear from the aligning of the timbers in the direction the sled is being drawn that the timbers are not rollers, but are there to give a timber-to-timber sliding contact.

Experiments to prove the efficacy of proposed methods of transporting and raising megaliths in ancient times have been reported over the years and some have formed the basis of television programmes. Many of these have taken little account of actual conditions, available materials and tools in ancient times and have not hesitated to use modern mechanical equipment when a difficult or quick lifting job was required. The most informative attempt in recent years relating to pyramid construction was the NOVA project, directed by archaeologist Mark Lehner and stonemason Roger Hopkins. Although attempting to rely as closely as possible on ancient techniques, the urgency demanded by a filming schedule necessitated the use of iron tools, not available to Old Kingdom builders, and a front end loader for placing the lower courses of stones. The experimental programme included both the use of levers and sleds for raising the 2 tonne stones. After exposing the deficiencies of the former, it was concluded that some system using a ramp or ramps was most likely to have been used. Similarly, the experiment showed up the problems of moving sled-mounted stones on rollers and came down in favour of a compacted roadbed with wooden cross-pieces, on which a 2 tonne stone could be pulled up a shallow incline by 20 men or fewer. The project obviously threw up a number of interesting facets which are often ignored, such as the difficulty of actually loading a stone block on to a sled.

Although sleds were undoubtedly known to the Egyptians in the Old Kingdom period, their use may have been restricted to special circumstances such as the moving of large awkwardly shaped objects, rather than for the rapid mass movement of stones required for the construction of the stone pyramids. Large numbers of men would have been needed to haul the sleds and even so the haulage rate would have been relatively slow. The need for specially prepared tracks with timber cross-pieces would have presented major problems within the quarries and even from the quarries to the site with so many stones, probably numbering a hundred or so, in transit at any given time. Even if some method could have been found to reduce the friction to very low values, this would have thrown up other problems, such as rendering the sled less stable; if the ropes broke or slipped on a ramp, the sled would have careered back down the slope, out of control. Manoeuvrability would have been a problem. The more tenable ramp solutions have the ramps spiralling around the pyramid, at least at the higher levels, but how could the haulers, numbering at least twenty and probably more, have pulled the sled around the corners? The only obvious answer would have been to lever it from behind, a slow laborious task completely out of keeping with the demanding logistics of the construction. One might also question how sled-mounted Tura stones could have been rapidly loaded on to barges to be taken across the Nile.

TEN

Rolling Stones

The demanding logistics of building the Great Pyramid could only have been met by a system which not only raised the stones, but also transported them to the site and across the working platform. While sleds might be regarded as a possible solution, they are inefficient, labour intensive and require carefully prepared tracks. In exploring the possibilities of an alternative method, it is instructive to consider the description of building the Great Pyramid given by Herodotus and to ask what precisely are the contrivances made of short pieces of timber that he claims were used to raise the stones. Certainly not levers, which are single, long pieces of timber. And not sleds, because he would have called a sled a sled. He simply did not know the name for these contrivances. The obvious candidate fitting this description is the cradle-like device, consisting of side pieces with curved undersides connected by an arc of dowels, many models of which Petrie found in the foundation deposits of Queen Hatshepsut's mortuary temple. He felt that prototypes of this

The quarter-circle shape of the cradle-like devices can be seen clearly in this example found by Petrie and now in the Cairo Museum.

device could have been used in the construction of the pyramids, but his suggestion of using it as a rocker is not tenable.

A close inspection of these cradle-like models, examples of which are now housed in both the Cairo Museum and the Metropolitan Museum of Art in New York, show the curvature of their under-sides to be quarter circles. The side pieces of a typical model in the Metropolitan Museum have heights of 52mm and lengths of 235mm, a ratio of 0.22. A true quarter circle has a ratio of 0.21, but taking into account the

These 0.4m long rods in the Cairo Museum may have been dowels from full-size cradles about 0.8m in length. The slight curvature on some may have been caused by pressure from the coiled rope.

slightly rounded ends of the side pieces of this particular model, the ratios correspond precisely. By fitting eight of these cradles on to a stone block, four near each end, it is possible to roll the block, which is a highly efficient way of moving it. If the Egyptian pyramid builders needed any convincing of this they had merely to watch the sacred scarab (dung) beetle rolling its dung food ball, often many times its own weight, along the ground, seeking a crevice or hollow in which to deposit it.

It can be shown by applying simple principles of mechanics (see Appendix) that rolling heavy objects is much easier than hauling them on a sled. In order to exploit this fundamental principle, however, it must be possible to convert the object

A dung beetle rolling its food ball. (*Corbis*)

into a circular or cylindrical form, capable of being rolled, and regular shaped blocks such as the pyramid stones lend themselves readily to this. It would be difficult, on the other hand, to convert awkwardly shaped objects such as statues into a form capable of being rolled.

Model tests have been performed by the writer to compare pulling a small concrete block, 107mm square by 210mm long and weighing 5.1kg (11.2lb), along a level surface and up a slope. A small wooden sled and wooden cradles were fashioned to fit the block. In each case the pulling force was applied through two cotton threads, thus limiting the maximum force that could be applied to 1.5kg (3.3lb). Tests

Sacred scarab
beetle rolling the
sun into the
Other World.

Pulling a sled carrying a model concrete block 107mm square and 210mm long, weighing 5.1kg. The coefficient of friction between the sled and smooth hardboard surface is 0.18 (static) and 0.16 (kinetic). The cotton threads have a combined strength of 1.5kg.

Cradle runners fitted to model concrete block to enable it to be rolled.

124

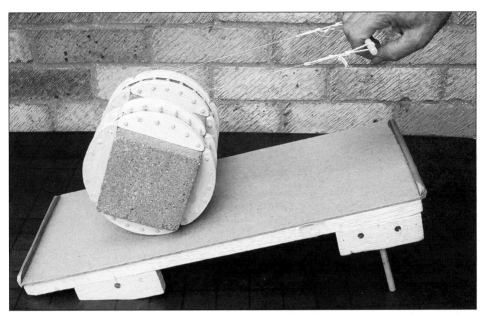

Rolling a 5.1kg block by means of two cotton threads up a 1 in 4 slope with a rough hardboard surface. The threads broke in the attempt to pull the block mounted on a sled up the same slope with a smooth surface.

Model block fitted with cradle runners held on 1 in 4 slope by wooden chocks. A sled on a slope smoothed to reduce friction cannot be held in this way and will slide uncontrollably down the slope.

were conducted on a level surface, a 1 in 10 slope (1 vertical to 10 horizontal) and a 1 in 4 slope. The surface itself consisted of hardboard, using the smooth side for the sled tests and the rough side for the rolling tests, the latter because rolling, unlike sliding, relies on a good frictional surface and indeed exploits the friction, which accounts in part for the greater efficiency of rolling (see Appendix).

The contact between the sled and the smooth hardboard gave a coefficient of static friction of 0.18 (i.e. pulling the sled from a stationary position) and a coefficient of kinetic friction of 0.16 (i.e., pulling the sled once in motion). Thus, the calculated force to pull the 5.1kg block from a stationary position on a level surface is 0.18 × 5.1kg, that is 0.92kg. As the cotton threads had a combined strength of 1.5kg it proved possible to pull the sled-mounted block along the level surface. Attempts to pull the block up a 1 in 10 slope had mixed results. The calculated resisting force is the frictional force of 0.92kg plus 0.51kg due to the slope, amounting to 1.43kg in total, only marginally less than the strength of the cotton threads. In some attempts it proved possible to pull the block up the slope, but in others the threads broke, probably reflecting some small variation in cotton strengths or slightly uneven distribution of pulling force between the two threads. When the sled was placed on a 1 in 4 slope the threads immediately broke and the sled slipped uncontrollably down the slope. Overall the sled tests confirmed very well the behaviour expected from the simple theory of mechanics.

A full-scale block fitted with cradle runners can be moved either by pushing from behind or by coiling ropes around the runners and pulling on the ropes. In the former case, according to the theory of mechanics, any force, no matter how small, should move the block on a level surface and the model tests confirmed the ease with which the block could be moved in this way. The coiled ropes would be used for pulling blocks up slopes, a method which the theory of mechanics shows to be much more efficient than using a sled (see Appendix), and this was confirmed by the model tests. Two coiled cotton threads around the runners pulled the block up a 1 in 4 slope very easily, confirming that the required force was less than 1.5kg, and in fact calculated to be 0.65kg. Pulling carefully to avoid jerking, it even proved possible to haul the block up the 1 in 4 slope with only one cotton thread, confirming that the force to be overcome was less than 0.75kg. These tests also confirmed an important safety feature of the rolling method by showing that the block could be held on the 1 in 4 slope by placing small wooden chocks behind it.

Encouraged by the success of the tests using models, a field programme was put in hand in Japan primarily to investigate the rolling of a 2.5 tonne block on a level surface and hauling it up a ramp with a 1 in 4 slope (see p. 167 for note on previous field tests). A 1 in 4 slope was chosen because in this author's view it is impossible to design a realistic ramp system with slopes flatter than this, which virtually rules out the use of sleds, with which negotiating slopes steeper than 1 in 10 would have been extremely difficult. Other investigations in the programme included fixing the cradles to the blocks, assessing the manoeuvrability of the cradle-mounted blocks and investigating the possibility of using the cradles with different shaped blocks. The bulk of the field programme, carried out at a site near Tokyo, was conducted on concrete blocks 0.8m square × 1.6m long and weighing 2.5 tonnes, thus

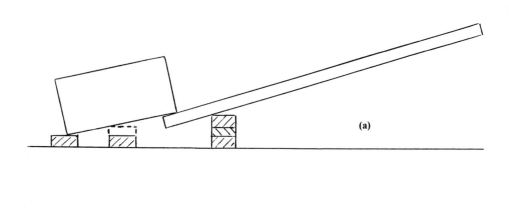

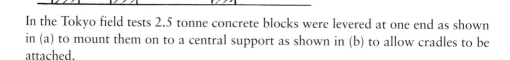

In the Tokyo field tests 2.5 tonne concrete blocks were levered at one end as shown in (a) to mount them on to a central support as shown in (b) to allow cradles to be attached.

corresponding to what is believed to be the average size of blocks in the Great Pyramid.

Fixing the cradles to a block involved three men, first levering the block from one end until it rested on a central block at sufficient height to allow cradles to be pushed under it at each end. The other cradles were then held in position to complete the circular runners and fixed tight to the block by encircling ropes around the cradles and tightening them against the cradle dowels. Up to 160m of hauling ropes were now wound around each cradle, giving a potential pull of 80m, as a rolling block moves 1m for every 2m of rope paid out.

Fitting cradles and coiled ropes to a 2.5 tonne concrete block with dimensions 0.8m square × 1.6m long. About 160m of rope could be wrapped around each runner, allowing the block to be pulled a possible distance of 80m before the ropes need to be rewrapped.

Tracks of lightly compacted and heavily compacted gravel were prepared to investigate what happened if the blocks were propelled along level surfaces with different degrees of preparation. These tests showed little variation in block behaviour on the two different surfaces and also demonstrated that a block could be rolled at a fast walking pace by two or three men pushing it from behind. It was an impressive sight to watch so few men propel with ease a 2.5 tonne block along a level surface; this was in stark contrast to the tests conducted by others (e.g. the NOVA project) using

Three men rolling a 2.5 tonne concrete block fitted with cradle runners on a level, lightly compacted gravel surface at a fast walking pace. The ropes are only required for negotiating slopes. About twenty men would have been needed to pull the same block over a level surface, which would also have needed special preparation to reduce friction, possibly by inserting timber cross-pieces into the road surface. As moving blocks from the quarries to the site was just as important as raising them, the ease of rolling, and the requirement of only minimum road surface preparation, would have given this method considerable advantage over the use of sleds.

sleds that needed not only greater surface preparation, but usually some form of wooden surface too, as well as around twenty men to haul. The Egyptians would surely have used this method of rolling to transport the blocks from quarry to site if they had known of the cradles at that time, as Petrie believed they did.

Rolling a 2.5 tonne concrete block up a 1 in 4 slope. Ten men were able to move the block a short distance and fourteen men could haul it up the full 15m ramp length, although up to twenty men were used. Between fifty and sixty men would have been required to haul the same sled-mounted block up this 1 in 4 slope.

Using the coiled ropes six men rolled the block easily up a 1 in 10 slope, which would have required up to thirty men hauling a sled, assuming each man capable of exerting a sustained pull of 36kg (80lb) and a coefficient of friction of 0.2, although it is unlikely that such a low value could have been achieved in the mass movement of stones required to construct the pyramids.

In tests conducted on the 1 in 4 slope, it was found that ten men, five on each rope, could move the block a short

ピッグプロジェクトと技術

Block nearing top of ramp. Note wooden chock hauled up behind block as a safety measure in case of rope breakage or slippage. A sled does not offer this safety feature, making it impossible to control if rope breakage or slippage did occur with a low friction surface.

distance and fourteen men could haul it up the full 15m ramp length, although in the interests of safety up to twenty men were used for some of the tests. Also, to ensure additional safety, a large baulk of timber was hauled up immediately behind the block to act as a chock in the unlikely event of rope slippage or breakage and, as part of the test programme, the block was brought to rest against the chock to show that it could be held safely on the slope. It proved possible to haul a block up the 15m ramp length in less than one minute, well within the time of less than five minutes felt necessary to meet the challenging logistics of constructing the Great Pyramid. The need to employ fourteen men to pull the block up the full length of the ramp indicates that on a slope of this steepness each man could sustain a pull of about 22.5kg (50lb), but could apply a pull of 32kg (70lb) when moving the block up in short stages. It also indicates that a sled-mounted block would have required over fifty men to haul it to the top even if a low coefficient of friction equal to 0.2 could have been achieved. However, this would have been a hazardous operation as any rope slippage or breakage would have resulted in the block careering out of control back down the slope.

Transportation of stones from the Tura quarries entailed loading them on to floating craft to cross the Nile. The task of loading and unloading the blocks on to and off the floating craft by rolling would have presented no great problem, unlike the use of sleds. By reversing the process of hauling blocks up the pyramid construction ramps, the blocks could have been lowered down ramps leading to the jetty, from which they would have been rolled along timber planks on to the craft and then easily rolled to their allocated place. Unloading would have involved a reversal of this procedure.

Left to itself on a flat surface a block fitted with cradles will roll uni-directionally, so methods have to be devised if it is wished to change its direction. The field tests showed that this can be done very easily: a small change in direction merely required two or three men to slew one end around slightly using levers; while a major change in direction, such as would be necessary on a spiral ramp wrapping around the corner of a pyramid, was achieved by four men rolling it on to a central block then swivelling it to assume its new direction.

Use of filling pieces of timber to accommodate cradles to block with rectangular shape.

On reaching the working platform, a block would have been rolled as close as possible to its final location and positioned on to a central support to allow the cradles to be removed. In a reversal of the procedure for attaching the cradles, the block would have been lifted slightly by levers enabling the support to be removed and then lowered by the levers on to the platform. It could then have been levered, pushed or bumped into its final position using heavy timber baulks, possibly sliding on a slick layer of wet mortar.

The field tests demonstrated that cradles could be fixed to blocks with rectangular, rather than square section, by the use of filling pieces of wood attached to the wider faces. This technique could be extended to accommodate more irregular

134

shapes by having different sizes of filling pieces and to blocks whose width and depth were less than the cradle length by having filling pieces attached to all four faces. Cradles attached to blocks with width and depth marginally longer than the cradles would still be effective, although giving a slight tumbling action. There is not likely to have been much need for this in constructing the Great Pyramid, because each layer, containing many thousands of blocks except in the very highest levels, had a uniform thickness, and many sets of cradles would have been needed as they would have worn out over time.

The transporting and raising of the massive granite beams over the King's Chamber, situated at mid-height of the Great Pyramid, presented a different problem to the limestone blocks. They were an order of magnitude larger in size; but each placement could be treated as a one-off operation, as they were few in number and speed of placement would not have been a factor. The largest beam has dimensions of 1.3m × 1.8m × 8.0m and weighs about 50 tonnes. With these dimensions it would have been possible to have fitted at least ten sets of cradles, and consequently to have had this number of pulling ropes. The Japanese tests showed that, by pulling in short stages and on a 1 in 4 slope, each man could exert a force of about 32kg, and it might be expected that the more experienced and trained Egyptian hauliers could have exerted pulls of short duration of 36kg or higher. Thus, the largest beam could have been hauled up a 1 in 4 ramp dedicated to beam raising, in short stages, chocking it after each pull while the men rested. This would have required about 160 men, or sixteen on each of ten ropes. Transportation to the site and across the working platform could have been achieved by

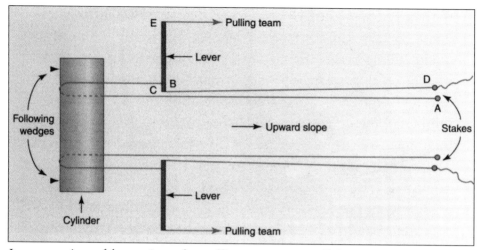

Incorporation of levers into the pulling system to roll heavy megalithic block (from J.H. Simpson, 'Further reflections on megalith mechanics', *Civil Engineering*, 144 (4), November 2001, 181–5, reproduced with the permission of the author and the Institution of Civil Engineers)

about sixteen men pushing from behind, or by using the ropes as necessary. It is impossible to imagine how these beams could have been raised by levers or sleds; the latter could have been hauled up 1 in 10 slopes by about 400 men, but it is difficult to imagine how a practical ramp system could have been built with slopes much less than 1 in 4, let alone as flat as 1 in 10.

It is possible that the number of men required to haul these huge blocks up the ramps could have been very much reduced by incorporating levers into the pulling system, as suggested by Harold Simpson for the haulage of Stonehenge sarsens. Although this would have greatly reduced the speed of haulage, and thus would not have been suitable, and indeed unnecessary, for the haulage of the limestone construction blocks, levers might well have been used to raise the beams for the tomb chamber, for which speed was not a factor. Simpson's method envisages rolling the blocks by means of parbuckling, but it could equally well have been adapted to coiled rope haulage. It could have reduced by perhaps four-fifths the number of men required to raise these massive beams.

ELEVEN

Ramps

There is no doubt that the ancient Egyptians made extensive use of ramps for raising stone blocks in their construction works, as witness, for example, the remains of a mudbrick ramp at Karnak, and it can be reasonably surmised that they employed a variety of materials for this purpose according to availability and circumstances. On completion of the structure the ramps would have been removed and the constituent material discarded or recycled in a nearby structure. Different ramp configurations may well have been used for different types of structure, and even for the same structures, Arnold making the point that the same ramp system may not have been employed for every pyramid project.

Many ramp systems have been suggested for the construction of the pyramids, most of them impracticable and some impossible. They fall into four broad categories: (1) ramps positioned at right angles to one or more of the pyramid faces; (2) ramps indented into one or more faces of the pyramid; (3) ramps erected within the interior of the pyramid;

and (4) ramps somehow attached to one or more faces of the pyramid. Of these, options (2) and (3) present major problems in finishing the pyramid; and while (1) might have been feasible for servicing the lower reaches of the major stone pyramids, it would have required vast amounts of ramp material and impossibly steep side slopes to reach the upper levels. Furthermore, each time the pyramid height rose by one layer of blocks, it would have been necessary to raise the ramp level and provide new surfacing.

A number of considerations might have influenced the design of the ramp system in the construction of a pyramid:

(1) The possibility of using locally available material, in most cases the surrounding desert sand and rubble.

(2) Keeping the volume of the ramp system to a minimum.

(3) Having ramp slopes compatible with the method adopted to raise the stones. Sleds would have needed slopes no steeper than about 1 in 10, whereas, with cradle runners fitted, stones could have been rolled up slopes of about 1 in 4.

(4) Providing a ramp surface suited to the method adopted to raise the stones. In the case of sled usage, this would have meant having timber pieces embedded into the surface to keep friction as low as possible by having timber-to-timber contact, while, for rolling stones, a lightly compacted surface would have sufficed, perhaps with a little gypsum cement to act as a binder.

(5) Ensuring the ramps had sufficient capacity to meet the construction logistics, notably the need to place, on average throughout the construction period, one stone every two minutes. This could only have been achieved by more rapid placement in the lower levels of the pyramid, probably at least one stone every minute. In this respect the pyramid shape was greatly advantageous in having the greatest part of its volume concentrated in the lower half. Two-thirds of the volume

Remains of
mudbrick ramp
at Karnak of
Romano-
Egyptian (XXX
Dynasty) age.

occupies the lowest one-third of the height, and 87 per cent occupies the lower half.

(6) In the case of the Great Pyramid, making provision for raising to mid-height the massive granite beams for the King's Chamber.

A ramp system for the Great Pyramid, suitable for rolling stones, could have consisted of sand and gravel from the surrounding desert, and possibly quarry chippings, in the lower portion, with stone ramps above this. The sand and gravel could have been placed against all four sides of the structure and allowed to lie at its angle of repose. Ramps of any chosen width could have been formed on top of this bank of material climbing up at slopes of 1 in 4 from each of the corners, against the pyramid face, making a total of eight ramps. By making ramps 6m in width, two blocks could have been hauled up alongside each other and also allowed room for descending hauliers carrying the cradles back to the quarries. With the completion of each pyramid layer, additional sand and rubble (gravel and chippings) would have been added and the ramps extended up to the next working platform; when the converging ramps on each face approached within about 20m of each other (end of Phase 1), the double ramp extensions would have ceased and one ramp on each face extended to the far corner (end of Phase 2). The 20m length was a minimum level working area allowing the blocks to be manoeuvred on to the working platform. Besides requiring a minimum of material, a major advantage of this type of ramp over a ramp at right angles to the pyramid face was the continual use throughout the construction of the same ramp surfaces, simply extending them in length with each rise in pyramid height.

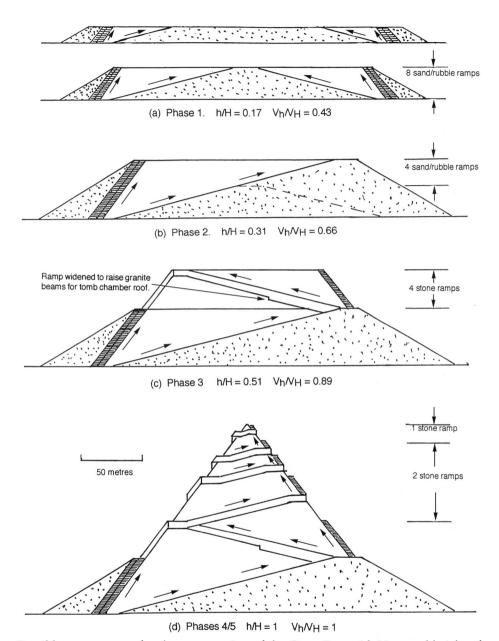

(a) Phase 1. $h/H = 0.17$ $V_h/V_H = 0.43$

8 sand/rubble ramps

(b) Phase 2. $h/H = 0.31$ $V_h/V_H = 0.66$

4 sand/rubble ramps

Ramp widened to raise granite beams for tomb chamber roof.

(c) Phase 3 $h/H = 0.51$ $V_h/V_H = 0.89$

4 stone ramps

50 metres

1 stone ramp

2 stone ramps

(d) Phases 4/5 $h/H = 1$ $V_h/V_H = 1$

Possible ramp system for the construction of the Great Pyramid. H = total height of pyramid; h = height at end of phase; V_H = total volume of pyramid; V_h = volume at end of phase.

143

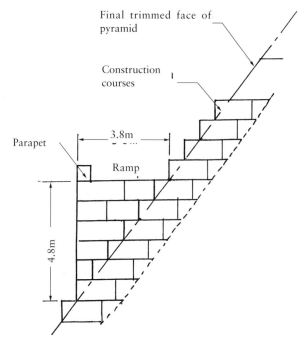

Final trimmed face of pyramid

Construction courses

3.8m

Parapet

Ramp

4.8m

Section through stone ramp resting on the outer steps of the pyramid, which were trimmed off, together with the ramps, in the final operation to complete the pyramid.

For the Great Pyramid, Phase 1 would have reached a height of about one sixth of the full pyramid height, but with 43 per cent of the stone, by volume, now having been rapidly placed with virtually unlimited ramp access. At the conclusion of Phase 2 the completed height for the Great Pyramid would have been about one third of the full height, with about 66 per cent of the full volume of blocks placed.

It would not have been practical to have raised the sand and rubble ramps for the Great Pyramid with slopes of 1 in 4 to heights greater than the end of Phase 2. An alternative form of ramp had to be adopted for the remaining height of the pyramid, but the problem was eased by the fact that 66 per cent of the masonry had already been placed at a rapid rate, so the number of haul tracks could be reduced. A credible solution would have been to erect stone ramps of single haul track width supported on the outer steps of the structure, which would have been removed after completion of the pyramid. The pyramids themselves are testimony enough to the skill of these ancient builders in erecting high quality masonry work, so construction of these ramps would not have presented them with any problems. The blocks for the ramps would have had to be trimmed carefully to size and possibly set with mortared joints. As with the sand and rubble ramps of Phases 1 and 2, these stone ramps would have been extended step by step as the structure rose, and at the current working level a temporary horizontal extension to each ramp, by some 5 to 10m, would have enabled the stones to be manoeuvred on to the working platform. As it approached within a few metres of the corner of the pyramid, each stone ramp would have been levelled off to allow the stones to be manoeuvred around it, a procedure found by the field tests in Japan to be easily achieved by four men rolling the stone on to a central support block and swivelling it. With the increasing height of the structure, the stone ramps would have been reduced in number from four (Phase 3), to two (Phase 4) and finally one (Phase 5) to the peak. At the end of construction the stone ramps would have been chipped away, together with the outer steps, to give a smooth face to each of the four sides of the pyramid.

As ramps were removed at the end of construction, there is little direct evidence of their usage or configuration. The remnant at Karnak is a rare example, but dates from very late in pharaonic times. One piece of evidence from the Old Kingdom period comes from Goneim who discovered and

Model of proposed ramp system for construction of the Great Pyramid. The lower sand portion, at its natural angle of repose, reaches to about one-third of the height of the completed structure, by which time in the pyramid itself the stones comprising two-thirds of the total volume would have been placed. The stone ramps serve only the top one-third of the pyramid volume. One sand ramp and an enlarged portion of stone ramp, as shown, could have been dedicated to raising the granite beams for the King's Chamber.

excavated the partially completed III Dynasty pyramid of Pharaoh Sekhemkhet. He found ramp material, consisting of 'chips of soft clay' obtained from the underground galleries, on all four sides of the structure, three of which he took to be for access of workmen on to the structure and the fourth for raising the stones. However, all four could have been used for raising stones; Goneim himself makes the point that the stones of the III Dynasty pyramids were small enough to be carried by two men. As the height of structure as found was only 7m,

146

about one-tenth of its intended height, it is impossible to predict how the ramp system may have developed as the structure rose.

There is a strong possibility that the mound of sand and rubble surrounding the Meidum Pyramid is the remains of a ramp system, similar to that proposed above, which was never removed because of the abandonment of the pyramid after its collapse at, or close to, the end of construction. If another pyramid had been constructed nearby this fill would no doubt have been re-used and thus removed from around the Meidum Pyramid; but this was never the case.

After studying the Meidum Pyramid for several years, Mendelssohn concluded that it had collapsed around the time of its completion and that the stones shed from its face formed the mound now surrounding it. However, much of the mound consists of sand and rounded river gravel identical to that of the desert surface all around the pyramid and is certainly not a product of decomposed limestone blocks. The substantial quantity of limestone chips found in the mound probably came from the quarries or the chipping of the outer stones to give the pyramid its smooth faces. It is likely that at the time of collapse the stones tumbled on to the sand and rubble ramp, and a small number can still be seen embedded in it. Petrie, who made extensive excavations in the mound in his search for the mortuary temple, noted that the pyramid functioned as the quarry for the whole area and that there were numerous tracks leading from it in all directions made by donkeys carrying the stones away. He even describes the method used to break up the stones to make them more portable. It is likely that the local people not only removed the stones resting on the ramps, but also any they could reach and remove from the

Allowing for much redistribution by wind and human activity, the mound at Meidum bears clear similarity to the lower portion of the proposed ramp in the model. The volume of the mound is less than it first appears, much of it being the lower intact portion of the pyramid, the face of which can be seen to the left.

The Meidum mound consists not of decomposed limestone blocks but mostly of desert sand and rounded gravel, and limestone chippings probably from the quarries and smoothing the pyramid faces. Local people removed the blocks which fell from the pyramid.

intact portion of the structure above the ramps, thus accounting for the observation made by Hart that the loss of stone is remarkably systematic on the four sides to have been caused by accident.

Allowing for redistribution of the mound material by the strong desert winds, graphically described by Petrie who was battered by 'air . . . full of whirling sand', and by the other innumerable excavations made in it over the millennia in attempts to discover its entrance and the mortuary temple, and

This modern ramp to the entrance climbs the mound against the face of the lower intact portion of the Meidum Pyramid.

even to make burials in the mound, the similarity to the sand and rubble portion of the ramp system, proposed here for rolling stones, is striking. It is interesting that even today a modern ramp used to reach the pyramid entrance rises up the mound against the intact lower portion of the pyramid exactly as proposed for the rolling stones. The first-century BC Greek historian Diodorus Siculus, who visited Egypt, claimed that the stones were raised on mounds, which could also be an interpretation of the ramp system proposed here.

TWELVE

The Workforce

It is widely accepted that Herodotus states it took 100,000 men twenty years to build the Great Pyramid, and while he may well have had this number in mind, he specifically relates it to the construction of the haulage road from the quarry to the construction site. In fact, with a total population of barely 1 million at that time the Egyptian economy could not conceivably have supported such a huge workforce; Herodotus may well have conjured up the number to impress his audience with the magnitude of the works, which he had seen and they probably never would. In asserting the use of an oppressed slave labour system he was simply echoing the words of the Egyptian priesthood, intent for their own reasons on giving Khufu a bad press. It is likely that impressed or corvée labour made up the bulk of the workforce and, indeed, it may have been considered something of an honour, or at least accepted as a civic duty, to work on the construction of the tomb for the god-king.

The system of corvée labour prevailed in Egypt until well into the nineteenth century, and was used by de Lesseps in the early stages of excavating the Suez Canal (commenced in 1859), until an international outcry and the need to speed up the work forced him to turn to mechanical excavators. Even if the priests had not emphasised the use of slave labour, Herodotus certainly would have, because his Greek listeners and readers could not have conceived of the construction of such massive works by any other method.

Based on his experience with the NOVA project, Lehner calculates that two crews of 2,000 men each could have accomplished the huge task of quarrying, hauling and setting the stones for the Great Pyramid. He further estimates that the total number building and maintaining the infrastructure of Khufu's pyramid could have been as high as 20,000 or even 25,000. This allows for construction of ramps and embankments (and presumably specially prepared haul tracks with timber cross-pieces for the sleds), as well as many ancillary and variously occupied workers such as carpenters and metal workers making and maintaining tools, sleds and other equipment. Bakers, brewers and suchlike are also included in this figure.

The rolling stone technique would not only have reduced considerably the number of men needed to transport and raise the stones (for example, three or four men could have rolled 2.5 tonne stones from the quarries to the pyramid site, compared to three or four times that number needed to haul a sled), but would also have required fewer men employed on haul track preparation and on the much simpler ramp system. However, the number of men employed in other activities such as quarrying (possibly peaking at 3,000 men; see Chapter 6), shaping and setting of stones, and various ancillary activities, would have been independent of those involved in hauling and raising the stones. Assuming the rolling technique was used, the total workforce at times of peak activity may have been around 15,000 and is unlikely to have exceeded 18,000.

The workforce was divided into gangs, and the numbers and sizes of the gangs would have been determined by the nature of the operations to which they were assigned. Graffiti found on pyramid stones attests to the workmen's pride in belonging to specific gangs, examples of which can be seen on stones fallen from the North Dahshur Pyramid on which are inscribed in red paint names such as the 'Green Gang' and the 'Western Gang'. This pride in gang membership would no doubt have been encouraged by those in charge to engender competition between gangs, leading to maximum output, the encouragement perhaps even extending to monthly rewards to the gangs achieving the best outputs for the period in their particular areas of responsibility. Where appropriate, several gangs may have worked together for specific tasks or, alternatively, a single gang may have been divided into sub-units: for example, four men could easily have rolled a 2.5 tonne stone across the Giza plateau from the quarry edge to the construction site, but larger numbers would have been required to move the stone up (or down) the quarry ramps to the quarry edge and to raise the stone up the pyramid ramps. Thus an efficient operation might have been achieved by a gang of twelve men first manoeuvring three stones to the quarry edge, dividing into three sub-units of four men each to convey the stones to the pyramid site, then reforming as a gang of twelve to raise the stones, individually, up the ramps to the working platform.

The workforce had to be housed, watered and fed, leading to the establishment of settlements – virtually towns – in close proximity to the construction site. As well as accommodation for staff and workmen, there would have been facilities for the storage of water and foodstuffs, for the manufacture of essential domestic items such as pottery and clothing, and probably workshops for the production and maintenance of tools used in the construction. Not surprisingly, there is evidence that the accommodation and living conditions for administrative staff, priests, supervisors and senior craftsmen were considerably superior to those of the general workforce. It is also possible that the former 'career' category remained on site permanently, whereas there may have been periodic turnover in all or part of the general impressed labouring force.

Although these settlements for the major stone pyramids must have been substantial and extensive, particularly at Dahshur and Giza, little evidence of their existence remains or has yet been found. Excavations by Mark Lehner in 1988–9 of a rectangular building with stone rubble walls and a floor of desert clay, which had been cleared out in the past, was revealing rather limited evidence of its usage when a mechanical backhoe, digging for sand nearby, gouged out a huge trench revealing thousands of potsherds from the pyramid age. Further examination of the trench by Lehner and his team unearthed two uncleared rooms with a layer of disintegrated mudbrick over black ash. The rooms had been bakeries. Embedded in the ash were vats for mixing dough and bell-shaped pots used for baking bread. Fish remains in a large mudbrick building adjoining the bakeries, together with the series of low shelves and troughs it contained, showed it to have been a fish processing plant in operation, like the bakeries, during the construction period of the pyramid for Menkaure.

The Lahun mudbrick pyramid built in the Fayum for Middle Kingdom pharaoh Sesostris II has undergone much greater degradation than the older stone pyramids, despite protective measures including outer limestone casing (probably quarried) and a surrounding drain for the rapid removal of water.

A more complete picture of a pyramid town has been revealed by Petrie's excavations at Kahun, mostly in 1888–90. Kahun accommodated the workforce engaged on the construction of the Lahun Pyramid for the Middle Kingdom pharaoh Sesostris II (sometimes called Senwroset II), who reigned 1897–78 BC. At this time the great hydraulic works and irrigation projects associated with the Fayum basin made it a focal point of Egyptian activity and it replaced Memphis as the administrative centre for the country. Sesostris II chose to site his pyramid close to the Bahr Yousuf canal linking the Nile to the Fayum near the modern village of Illahun. This pyramid, with base lengths of 106m, a height of 48.6m and slopes slightly steeper than 42°, was one of a number of large mudbrick pyramids of Middle Kingdom age. The builders took advantage of a natural, 12m high core of rock, radiating from which they constructed a series of limestone walls linked by cross-walls, the spaces between which they filled with mudbrick and above which they placed mudbrick to complete the structure. Measures to protect the mudbrick from the elements included outer limestone casing (which has no doubt been quarried) and a surrounding rubble-filled trench to collect and rapidly dispose of water running off the face of the pyramid. Despite these measures, the structure is now much degraded.

It is uncertain to what extent the arrangements for accommodating and feeding the much smaller workforce for a Middle Kingdom mudbrick pyramid mirrored those for an Old Kingdom stone pyramid. In one respect at least Kahun would have been similar to the earlier pyramid towns – in its division into separate walled off areas for officials and priests on the one hand and the general workforce on the other. The humble

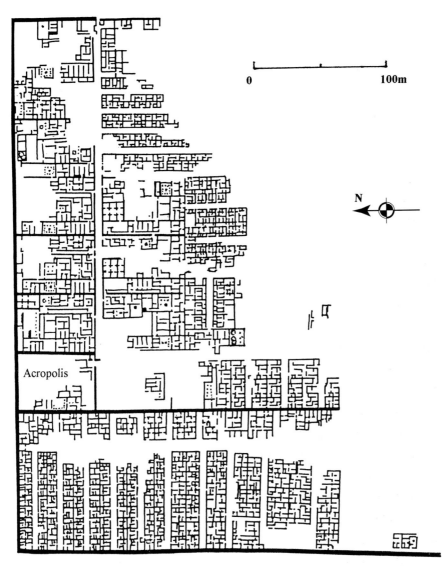

The walled pyramid town of Kahun in the Fayum, built to serve the workforce for the mudbrick pyramid of the Middle Kingdom pharaoh Sesostris II (1897–78 BC), was excavated by Petrie in 1888–90. It was divided physically into a western section with rows of houses for the workmen and the eastern portion, much larger in area, containing the mansions of the nobility and high officials overseeing the work. Similar arrangements no doubt pertained during the construction of the much earlier stone pyramids.

159

dwellings of the workmen occupied the western portion of the town, some 3.5 hectares in area, while the eastern portion, nearly three times the size, provided lavish housing for priests and senior officials. One prominent walled off area in the north-western corner of the eastern sector, situated on a raised knoll of rock known as the 'acropolis', may have housed the king himself. The walls of the houses, mostly one-storey in height, were constructed of mudbrick; and the flat roofs, accessible by steps, consisted of wooden beams supporting poles to which bundles of reeds or straw were bound and mud plaster applied to the inner and outer surfaces. Rooms in some houses were roofed with mudbrick barrel vaulting. Baked brick tiles paving the alleys separating the housing blocks sloped downward in order to shed water into stone channels that ran down the middle of each street.

The western portion of the town consisted of tightly packed rows of houses, with the number of rooms in the houses ranging from three to six or higher. For ease and speed of construction the builders adopted repetitive plans, with standard length units of 2, 3, 4, 5 and 10 cubits (one cubit equals approximately 0.5m). Complete with kitchens, some with facilities for grain storage, these houses clearly catered for workmen, and maybe lesser officials, with their families, and not for single men. Perhaps remains of such accommodation have not survived or were not revealed by the excavations, which left a substantial part of the town's remains untouched. The logic and logistics of providing accommodation and food suggest that the bulk of the much larger workforces employed on the major stone pyramids must have been single men housed in barrack-like structures, perhaps in groups of a dozen or so, each served by one man who maintained the accommodation, secured provisions from central stores and cooked for his group.

The nobility and high-ranking officials overseeing the building of the Lahun Pyramid did not stint themselves in their accommodation or lifestyle, and no doubt this was true, too, in the construction of the stone pyramids. The mansions in the eastern portion of Kahun bore no relationship to the humble quarters of the workmen, separated physically only by a stone wall, but by an unscalable mountain range in terms of lifestyle. Living areas in these mansions equalled fifteen to twenty times the area occupied by an average workman's family, and up to fifty times the smaller units, with reception rooms and passages leading to private family rooms, business rooms and servants' quarters.

In addition to their much superior accommodation, it is safe to assume that the nobility and high-ranking officials enjoyed more varied meals than did the bulk of the workforce, whose staple diet, as with most Egyptians at the time, would have consisted of bread and beer, both made from the grains of barley or emmer wheat. After kneading and mixing yeast, milk, salt and spices into the flour, the dough could have been formed into simple dollops and baked on a heated kitchen slab. On the other hand, based on finds made in the excavated Giza bakeries, Lehner suggests that the bread may have been mass produced by pot baking, each resulting loaf, heavy in starch and calories, sufficing one man for several days. Fish may have been a staple form of protein and, less commonly, meat, probably in the form of stew.

There would have been no shortage of vegetables for the stew, or to eat separately or, in the case of beans, prepared as a purée for spreading on the bread to make it more appetising.

A simple snack for eating during the day at the construction site or in the quarry might have consisted of bread and onions, together with goat's milk, well curdled and salted. An interpreter drew the attention of Herodotus to an inscription on one of the lower stones of the Great Pyramid recording that the authorities spent 1,600 talents of silver on radishes, onions and leeks for the workforce, and he goes on to speculate, on this evidence, about the large amounts that must have been spent on bread and clothing for the labourers during all the years of building.

While the nobility and high-ranking officials would have had a choice of drink with their meals, including a variety of wines grown in different parts of the country, the workmen would have had their dark and nutritious, but only mildly alcoholic, beer, the sugar content of which could have been raised by the addition of date juice. Diodorus, whose natural drink would have originated from the grape, found Egyptian beer not much inferior in taste and savour to that of wine.

Closing Remarks

The idea of rolling heavy objects is not new. No one would drag a heavy cylindrical object when it can be so much more easily rolled and, indeed, men have been rolling heavy caskets of ale for centuries and lowering them down ramps into cellars by looping ropes around them and paying them out gradually – a process known as parbuckling. In his book *The Stones of Stonehenge*, published in 1924, Herbert Stone showed by model tests how, by attaching shaped pieces of timber to them, the 10 tonne lintels at Stonehenge could have been rolled up ramps by parbuckling to rest on top of the upright sarsens.

The earliest written account of the rolling of large stone blocks seems to be that by the first-century AD Roman engineer-cum-architect Vitruvius. He first describes the efforts of Chersiphron and his son Metagenes in the sixth century BC to transport, respectively, shafts and architraves from the stone quarries some 13km to the temple of Diana at Ephesus. Chersiphron devised a frame consisting of two longitudinal pieces of timber, linked by cross-pieces at the ends fitted with rings at their mid-lengths to receive iron stub axles fixed to the ends of the circular shafts. The shafts were rotated, and hence rolled over the underlying surface, by oxen pulling on ropes attached to the timber frame. Metagenes enclosed the ends of the rectangular-shaped architraves in 3.6m diameter circular timber structures described by Vitruvius as 'wheels' so that they would roll, then adopted the same method as his father to roll the stones from the quarries to the temple site. Vitruvius describes the topography over which the stones were rolled as an uninterrupted plain. Over a flat, horizontal surface, the axial pull adopted by Metagenes and his father would have been almost as effective as a peripheral pull, but required the fixing of stub axles to the stones, which would have introduced the additional problem of axle friction and the need for some form of lubrication to reduce this.

The other case cited by Vitruvius concerns one Paconius, who lived around the time of Vitruvius, and who was contracted to cut a 40 tonne stone block in the same Ephesus quarries and transport it to the site of the temple of Apollo, to replace the cracked pedestal supporting a large statue of the god. He enclosed each end of the block in circular timber 'wheels' and connected the rims of these with closely spaced timber bars, effectively encapsulating the block in a wooden cylinder, which could be rolled. According to Vitruvius, 'Then he [Paconius] coiled a rope round the bars, yoked up his oxen, and began to draw on the rope'. Paconius failed in his attempt as the stone swerved off course, probably as a result of using only a single rope, which would have given him little control over its direction, exacerbated by the fact that the rope, rather than the timber bars, was in contact with the ground. The Egyptian cradles were cleverly designed to have their dowel arcs inset, so that the rims of the cradle runners and not the rope contacted the ground. Moving heavy stone blocks by rolling may have been quite common in the ancient world, but Paconius, having heard of it, simply failed to apply the principle successfully.

In early 1995, going through literature on the construction of the pyramids as part of my more general interest in the history of civil engineering, I came across an illustration of the cradle-like devices discovered by Petrie in the foundation deposits of Hatshepsut's mortuary temple. I was immediately convinced these were quarter circles and might well have been used in the construction of the pyramids, as suggested by Petrie, but in a way very different to that he had envisaged.

My review of the literature on ancient Egypt, and the pyramids in particular, at that time turned up a number of references to these devices, together with sketches and photographs, but invariably echoing Petrie's suggestion of their possible usage as rockers to raise the pyramid stones. The one exception I found suggested that by mounting the stones on them it would have made dressing them easier. I followed this review by carrying out the model tests described in this book, which demonstrated, as anticipated from the basic laws of mechanics, that rolling blocks fitted with cradle runners was much more efficient than sliding sled-mounted blocks, and required much less force. These model tests were described in a Cambridge University Engineering Department report in 1995.

In October 1995, I visited Egypt and after a long search found one of these devices in an odd corner of the Cairo Museum. Most of them are, in fact, in the Metropolitan Museum of Art in New York. At this time I discussed my ideas with two leading Egyptologists in Cairo, neither of whom knew of any previous proposals to use these devices as a means of rolling the pyramid stones.

In December 1995, while attending a conference on geotechnical engineering in Cairo, I was invited to give a talk to a varied audience, many of them engineers, on the construction of the pyramids. After the talk, a leading Japanese geotechnical engineer, Professor Tom Kimura, thought one of the large Japanese civil engineering contractors might be interested in conducting full-scale experiments. On returning to Japan, he found that the Obayashi Corporation was indeed receptive to the idea, and experiments were conducted at a site near Tokyo in September 1996. My principal aim in these experiments was to show that 2.5 tonne concrete blocks could easily be rolled up a 1 in 4 slope, as I could not (and still cannot) envisage a practical ramp system for the construction of the Great Pyramid having slopes much flatter than this. The experiments were a success and also showed up several other interesting points relating, for example, to manoeuvrability, safety and, not least, the ease with which the blocks could be rolled along a lightly compacted level track by two or three men. A brief account of these tests was given in an article to *ATSE Focus*, published by the Australian Academy of Technological Sciences and Engineering, January/February 1997.

In March 1997, I was invited to give a talk as part of National Science Week in Cambridge. This talk attracted a record audience of about 650, reflecting the widespread interest in subjects relating to the pyramids. I have since repeated this talk, and derivatives from it, in a number of countries, to a variety of audiences.

Shortly after my Cambridge talk, in the Cambridge University Library I came across a book by Lepre, which I had missed in my earlier review of the literature. It is essentially a catalogue of the many pyramids in Egypt, but tucked away in an appendix is an account of various proposals for their construction. These include a brief description of tests made in Boston in 1980 by an American engineer, John Bush, who realised that the cradle-like devices were quarter circles. Unfortunately, little detail is given of the tests, other than the fact that 2.5 tonne blocks with cradles attached were rolled up ramps. The ramp slopes are not given, but were clearly flatter than 1 in 4 as only six men were hauling the blocks. Lepre describes these tests as 'impressive', but dismisses the method as unlikely to have been used to construct the pyramids on the curious basis that holes in the sides of the cradles made by Bush to take ropes securing the cradles to the blocks are not present in the models. As these are only models this seems of little consequence and, in any case, there are other means of securing the cradles to the blocks, as shown by the tests in Japan. Lepre favours the sled to transport the blocks to the site and to place the lowest five pyramid layers, and a strange double fulcrum lever mechanism to lift stones above this level. For whatever reason – and Lepre's dismissal of the method may have contributed – the tests by John Bush have received very little publicity and are either unknown to Egyptologists or have been ignored by them in favour of other methods, usually sleds or levers, or both.

In 1999, while browsing in the Cambridge market, I found a second-hand paperback entitled *A History of the Machine* by Sigvard Strandh, with an illustration of the cradle-like devices attached to a block, attributed to a 'recently published theory', proposing that the pyramids could have been rolled 'to their destination' in this way. No information is given on where the theory was published, or who proposed it. The paperback version of the book, which I bought for £2, was published in 1984, but the original Swedish version and its English translation were published in 1979, and thus pre-date the Boston tests. As these devices have been known for over 100 years it is possible that there have been even earlier proposals, either not published or only to be found in obscure publications, suggesting their use in the way put forward here.

On my visit to the Cairo Museum earlier in 2003, I found three of these cradle-like devices displayed and labelled as 'bascules'. *Chamber's Dictionary* defines 'bascule' as 'an apparatus of which one end rises as the other end sinks', clearly reflecting Petrie's suggested usage. Petrie, on this occasion, was wrong. Used as a means for rolling the stone blocks to construct the stone pyramids, it reduced by up to 80 per cent the manpower required to achieve this task. It is unlikely that the major stone pyramids could have been built without it, as the manpower requirements of any other method would have placed an intolerable burden on the country's rural economy. In brief, it was a remarkable technological step forward. A great Egyptian invention. It should be acknowledged as such.

APPENDIX

Sliding and Rolling – Some Simple Mechanics

Dragging or rolling were the only options available to the builders of the IV Dynasty pyramids, capable both of transporting the stones from the quarries and of raising them to their designated destinations in the structures. According to Goneim, the relatively small stones in the III Dynasty pyramids could have been lifted by manpower alone, without the need for mechanical aid. Conceptually, sleds could have been dragged along a prepared surface, possibly lubricated or consisting of embedded timber pieces, or they could have been mounted on rollers. A stone converted by suitable attachments to a cylindrical form could have been fitted with stub axles at either end and the pull applied to the axles, or it could have been rolled by pushing from behind or by a peripheral pull delivered through a rope looped or coiled around the cylinder. These possibilities are shown in Figure A1. The calculated forces required to move blocks with all-up weight W by these different methods along a level surface and up slopes of 1 in 10 and 1 in 4 are given in Table A1 below. It is assumed here that the prepared tracks along which the blocks are drawn are sufficiently firm to ensure that traction forces, resulting from small displacements of the track surface, are negligible. The rolling cylinders are assumed to be centrally balanced.

Appendix

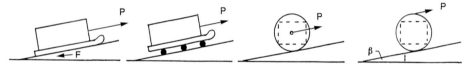

Figure A1. Possible methods for transporting and raising heavy stone blocks.

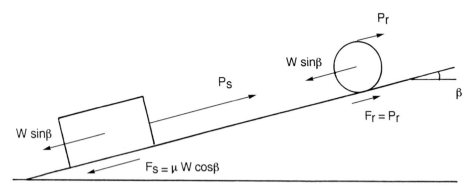

Figure A2. Forces parallel to slope with angle β, where W is weight of block, P_s, P_r are required pulling forces for sliding and rolling respectively and F_s, F_r are corresponding friction forces.

Table A1 Forces required to move blocks by different methods along various surfaces

Hauling method		Pulling force		
	General	$\beta = 0$	$\beta = 1$ in 10	$\beta = 1$ in 4
Sled	$\mu W\cos\beta + W\sin\beta$	0.20W*	0.30W*	0.44W*
Sled on rollers	$W\sin\beta$	0	0.10W	0.24W
Rolling-axial pull	$W\sin\beta$	0	0.10W	0.24W
Rolling-peripheral pull	$0.5W\sin\beta$	0	0.05W	0.12W

Key
* Coefficient of friction μ assumed = 0.20
W = all-up weight

Appendix

The force required to pull a sled-mounted block with all-up weight W along a hard, flat, horizontal surface is μW, where μ is the coefficient of friction between the sled and the underlying surface, while, in theory, any finite force, no matter how small, would move the block utilising any of the other three methods. The actual forces required using any of these three methods will not be zero, but depend on factors such as the alignment of rollers under a sled and the ability to control them, balance of rolling stones and axle friction in the case of axial pull. Nevertheless, the remarkable ease with which a 2.5 tonne block was rolled along a level, lightly compacted surface in the Tokyo tests confirms the general correctness of these theoretical conclusions.

On a slope of 1 in 10, the peripherally pulled rolling block requires a pull of only one-sixth of that for a sled and half that for the other two methods, but it is questionable whether a practical ramp system could have been built with such flat slopes for the construction of the major stone pyramids. It would have been virtually impossible to pull sled-mounted blocks up ramps steeper than this, having regard to the need for rapid placement of stones, while the difficulty of controlling rollers under sleds on the level are multiplied several times on sloping ramps.

The great advantage of rolling stones with a coiled rope comes from the fact that slopes of 1 in 4 could be negotiated, making possible a highly practical ramp system. Tests with models, and the Tokyo field tests, have confirmed the ease with which heavy stones can be rolled up slopes of this steepness. As shown in Table A1, the force required to pull a stone up a slope is at least 50 per cent less than for any other method, and the reduction is much greater compared to a sled. On a 1 in 4 slope the calculated force required for rolling a block by coiled rope is little more than a quarter of that required for a sled and, perhaps even more tellingly, the force required to roll a block up a slope of 1 in 4 is 60 per cent less than that required to haul a sled-mounted block up a much flatter slope of 1 in 10.

Appendix

A physical explanation of why the peripheral pull rolling technique up a slope is much more efficient than the sled is illustrated in Figure A2, which depicts the forces parallel to the slope. While the friction between sled and ramp acts against the pulling force, the friction between the rolling block and ramp acts in the direction of the pulling force and provides half the required up-slope force.

Select Bibliography

Andreu, Guillemette. *Egypt in the Age of the Pyramids*, London, John Murray, 1997

Arnold, D. *Building in Egypt – Pharaonic Stone Masonry*, New York, Oxford University Press, 1991

Baines, J. and Malek, J. *Atlas of Ancient Egypt*, Facts on File, Oxford, 1992

Bauval, R. and Gilbert, A. *The Orion Mystery*, London, Heinemann, 1994

Borchart, I. *Die Entstehung der Pyramide*, Berlin, Springer Verlag, 1928

Choisy, A. *L'Art de Bâtir Chez les Egyptiens*, Paris, 1904

Clarke, S. and Engelbach, R. *Ancient Egyptian Masonry*, London, Oxford University Press, 1930

Cotterell, B. and Kamminga, J. *Mechanics of Pre-Industrial Technology*, Cambridge, Cambridge University Press, 1990

David, A.R. *The Pyramid Builders of Ancient Egypt*, London, Routledge & Kegan Paul, 1986

Edwards, I.E.S. *The Pyramids of Egypt*, Harmondsworth, Penguin, 1961

Fahkry, A. *The Pyramids*, Chicago, University of Chicago Press, 1961

Goneim, M.Z. *The Buried Pyramid*, Longmans, Green & Co., 1956

Hart, G. *Pharaohs and Pyramids*, London, Herbert Press, 1991

Hayes, W.C. *The Sceptre of Egypt*, New York, Metropolitan Museum of Art, 1953

Herodotus. *The Histories*, trans. Aubrey de Selincourt, Harmondsworth, Penguin, 1954 (revd edn by A.R. Burn, 1972)

Hodges, P. *How the Pyramids Were Built*, Warminster, Aris & Phillips Ltd, 1993

Kerisel, J. *Down to Earth*, Rotterdam, Balkema, 1987

——. *Genie et Demesure d'un Pharaon: Kheops*, Editions Stock, 1996

Lehner, M. *The Complete Pyramids*, London, Thames & Hudson, 1997

Lepre, J.P. *The Egyptian Pyramids*, McFarland, 1990

Lucas, A. *Ancient Egyptian Materials and Industries*, London, Edward Arnold, 1954

Mendelssohn, K. *The Riddle of the Pyramids*, London, Thames & Hudson, 1974

Parry, R.H.G. 'Rolling Stones', *ATSE Focus*, Australian Academy of Technological Sciences and Engineering, No. 95, January/February 1995

——. 'Megalith Mechanics', *Civil Engineering* 138, Proceedings of the Institution of Civil Engineers, November 2000

Partridge, R. *Transport in Ancient Egypt*, London, Rubicon, 1996

Petrie, W.M.F. *The Pyramids and Temples of Gizeh*, London, 1883

——. *Illahun, Kahun and Gurob*, London, 1891

——. *Medum*, London, David Nutt, 1892

——. *Arts and Crafts of Ancient Egypt*, London, Foulis, 1910

Simpson, H. 'Further Reflections on Megalith Mechanics', *Civil Engineering* 144 (4), Proceedings of the Institution of Civil Engineers, November 2001

Strandh, S. *A History of the Machine*, New York, A & W Publishers, 1979

Vitruvius. *The Ten Books of Architecture*, trans. Morris Hickey Morgan, London, Constable & Co., 1914

Index

Index